The
COUNTRY COUSINS'
Christmas Collection

The
COUNTRY COUSINS' CHRISTMAS COLLECTION

34 short stories about family, faith, and fun

KONNIE MEYER

Cover illustration by eleven year old, Evelyn May (Evie) Meyer

XULON PRESS

Xulon Press
2301 Lucien Way #415
Maitland, FL 32751
407.339.4217
www.xulonpress.com

© 2021 by Konnie Meyer

All rights reserved solely by the author. The author guarantees all contents are original and do not infringe upon the legal rights of any other person or work. No part of this book may be reproduced in any form without the permission of the author.

Due to the changing nature of the Internet, if there are any web addresses, links, or URLs included in this manuscript, these may have been altered and may no longer be accessible. The views and opinions shared in this book belong solely to the author and do not necessarily reflect those of the publisher. The publisher therefore disclaims responsibility for the views or opinions expressed within the work.

Paperback ISBN-13: 978-1-66283-126-3

Dedication

This book is lovingly dedicated to Bruce,
my husband of almost fifty years,
and our nine active grandchildren,
AKA the Country Cousins:
Mack, Gus, Evie, Meyta, Cece,
Bo, Malone, Larkin, Ike
AND
their parents.

Special Recognition

Thanks to Dave for introducing me
to the Black Swamp Writers' Guild of
Ottawa, Ohio. With a special
"shout out" to Bette and Nancy.
YOU ALL ARE THE BEST!

"The most time-honored gift you can give
your children and grandchildren are forever memories
in the form of written family stories."
Konnie Meyer

Table of Contents

Preface xi

Caught Cat Napping 1
Game Day Granny 7
Ultimate Wish Book 13
Sneak Peak 19
Pass the Pizza, Please! 25
Canine Conspiracy 31
Letter to Santa 37
Hide-and-Seek 45
Evening in Paris 49
Real Deal 55
Potluck Panic 61
Table-time 67
Silent Night 73
Holiday Superheroes 79
Miraculous Scotch Tape 85

Savor the Season 91

Christmas Correspondence 97

Follow-the-Leader 103

Time Travelers. 109

Christmas Truce 115

Family Gathering Part I. 121

Family Gathering Part II. 127

Pocketknife Possibilities 135

Guilty as Charged. 141

Kitchen Cowgirl. 145

Wedding Wisdom 151

My Version of an Excursion 157

Penny Power 163

Trash Talk. 169

TV Transformation 175

Action or Inaction? 181

Go With the Flow 187

Soup Surprise! 193

A Laughing Matter. 199

Preface

If you're wondering about this book and its title, let me explain. I'm a gray-haired grandma/retired teacher/farm wife. Unlike some women, I don't particularly enjoy baking or cooking. Consequently, I have no special recipes or culinary skills to pass on to my heirs. So, listen up, grandkids! If there's a future Rachael Ray or Wolfgang Puck among you, I can only offer moral support. Likewise, my crocheting and sewing skills are nonexistent. As a result, there will be no Afghan blankets or cuddly quilts bequeathed to my beloved grandbabies. Forget gardening or playing cards; my grandkiddos can't count on me for guidance or participation here either.

As you can see, my talents are limited. This presents a problem. What will be my legacy? What lasting gift can I give these Country Cousins; AKA my nine grandchildren? I'd like to think there's at least one thing I've become moderately good at and that's sharing stories. Over time, memories fade. There are no guarantees my grandkids will remember tales told at family get-togethers. As a result, I've made it my mission to write it all down; to chronicle what I remember and what I've observed. My goal is to paint a panoramic picture with words - a lasting portrait of our family's history - a history that will continue to be shared. (At least, that's my plan.)

For this Country Cousin collection, I've chosen to focus on the Thanksgiving/Christmas/New Year season. The family stories are true, and I hope you enjoy reading my tales of tribute to the holidays as much as I enjoyed bringing them together for this book.

Preface

As the old saying goes, "If the good Lord's willing and the creek don't rise," there could be more Country Cousin Collections. For now, Merry Christmas and Happy Reading!

Caught Catnapping

To some kids, nighttime is when you get your second wind, that sudden spurt of energy, which could easily propel you through to midnight, if only your parents would allow that to happen. On our family picture wall is an old black-and-white photo of me, taken when I was two. I'm standing on the stairway, sobbing. Was I hurt? Had I been scolded? Was I sick? Had some traumatic event occurred, causing the flood gates to open? The answer to all these questions is a resounding "No!" I'm crying simply because I didn't want to go to bed.

Back then, I can remember absolutely hating sleep of any kind, naps included. I especially hated it when my parents napped on Sunday afternoons, and I certainly never wanted to "just settle down and rest," as my dear, no doubt sleep-deprived mother often suggested. Now, some sixty-eight years later, I look at that picture and say to myself, "What was I thinking? Naps are needed! Naps are necessary! Naps are nice!" Now I can honestly declare, "I LOVE NAPS!"

Several years ago, after Thanksgiving, my husband, Bruce, our youngest daughter, Ali, and I drove to Columbus, Ohio to Christmas shop at the Tuttle Mall. While my daughter and I looked for the nearest shoe store, my husband looked for the nearest coffee kiosk where he could sit and "people watch." To him, shopping is a form of torture, which is why I usually buy his clothes, bring them home, let him choose, then return whatever he doesn't want. No fuss, no muss, and no shopping on his part. I guess you could call it his own personal version of the "Home Shopping Network."

We assured him we'd check back in an hour and drop off any of our purchases for him to guard. When we returned, he wasn't at the kiosk. A quick look around showed no sign of him. Where, oh where, was my hubby hiding? This was way back in the dark ages, the time called B.C., meaning <u>B</u>efore <u>C</u>ell phones, so we had no way of contacting him. Our search began.

Well, it didn't take us long to spot him in a middle aisle, stretched out on the first of four La-Z-Boy recliners. They were apparently on sale as part of a holiday promotion. There he was, my practically comatose partner, head back, feet up, mouth wide open, snoring loudly while bright lights shined down, and busy shoppers swirled all around him. I guess he got comfortable and figured nobody in

Columbus would recognize him, so he took a catnap.

Staring down at him, we couldn't decide if he reminded us of Sleeping Beauty or Rip van Winkle. Either way, neither of us wanted to claim him; so we took our bags, leaving him in his own personal lullaby land. An hour later we returned to the original kiosk where we found him wide awake, well rested, sipping coffee, ready and willing to protect our packages. Looking back, I think he should have gotten a stipend for his reality recliner endorsement.

Unfortunately, some things never change. I still don't like to "call it a day" and go to bed at night. Consequently, I've been known to wake up at dawn only to discover I was snoozing the night away in my La-Z-Boy recliner while still in my clothes. On these occasions, I have flashbacks to our Christmas shopping episode at the mall.

Caught Catnapping

Fortunately, some things do change. Over the years I've learned to embrace daytime naps. There's a lot to be gained from taking a little catnap now and then. I'm sure my husband will vouch for that. Hmmm, I've been thinking. This story is finished. Lunchtime is over. Maybe I'll head to the recliner, kick back, and close my eyes. "Sweet dreams, everyone!"

Gameday Granny

Football enthusiasts across the country are familiar with the gridiron rivalry sandwiched between Thanksgiving and Christmas. Yes siree, this is the time when Ohio State Buckeyes face Michigan Wolverines in their legendary border battle. But, for the Country Cousin clan, this one particular gameday was unlike any other.

We prepared for this special event by purchasing beverages, snacks, and necessary paper products. After stuffing four separate minivans to the brim with kids, dogs, and goodies, we headed to our separate, side-by-side mini cottages at Hamilton Lake, Indiana.

Proudly wearing Buckeye shirts and hats, we arrived Friday afternoon with lots of time to spare before "kick off" on Saturday. We unpacked, tested the television reception, went out for a yummy supper at Roger's Harvest House (the local diner) and returned to the cottages to relax. So far, so good! It's nice when things go as planned, but you and I both know, that's not always how life works.

Sure enough, when Saturday morning rolled around, I got a message from my middle daughter, Anita, saying she and her husband, Bryan, had a "really rough night!" For the past ten hours they had been waging their own battle. Shared texts indicated their gastrointestinal discomfort was attributed to possible food poisoning from a Thanksgiving brunch eaten the morning before. Fortunately their three kiddos were fine, but obviously the parents needed quiet and rest.

I quickly formulated an alternate gameday game plan. I suggested we split the eight grandkids into teams. The two oldest boys, Mack and Gus, could stay and watch the game. The two toddlers, Malone and Larkin, would hopefully take a long nap. I "recruited" the middle four, Evie, Meyta, Cece, and Bo, ages four through nine, to go shopping with me in nearby Angola. (At this time, the youngest cousin, Ike, was just a glimmer in his parents' eyes.)

Before anyone could say "coin toss," we were on our way. To ring in the Christmas season, the kiddie quartet belted out lyrics to "Rudolph the Red Nosed Reindeer." Guess Ohio State's fight song was not yet in their repertoire, but I soon discovered "**O–H!**" "**I–O!**" was a chant all four of them knew.

Our first stop was the toy section at Kohls. Sporting her Ohio State jersey, Quarterback Granny called an "audible" at the "line of scrimmage." "Listen up, you Country

Cousins! We're a team, so stick together like glue. You can each pick one small toy. Remember to focus on the word, SMALL. Help each other out. Let's put our hands together, and on the count of three say, Go Buckeyes!"

After scoring "touchdowns" in the toy section, Coach Granny grabbed her clipboard and herded her Country Cousin team to the little-boy-coat-area. The desired, size five, hooded coat was naturally eight feet up, hanging at the tip-top of a wall rack. Coach Granny called, "time out" to get help. With no clerk in sight, a long metal rod was spotted and used to retrieve the coat. Bo put it on.

"Good fit! Good zipper! I like it! I'll wear it!" cheered the enthusiastic cousin as he yanked off the price tags. Referee Granny blew her whistle and called, "illegal motion!" "You can't wear it until it's paid for," she said, while teammate Cece quickly "intercepted" the tags, shoving them in the coat pocket for safe keeping. The three girls each picked out a nightgown, thankfully leaving the price tags attached.

Our "half time" entertainment consisted of pushing buttons to test multiple functions of floor-model massage chairs. Finally leaving that "playing field" behind, we decided to visit a game day concession stand. This Granny watched helplessly as all four hand-holding cousins slipped on the restaurant's freshly mopped floor, landing in a giggling heap just past the entryway. Luckily, nobody was injured on that "tackle."

After finishing ice-cream treats, we headed home. Before climbing out of the "team bus," the four Country Cousins listened to Coach Granny's final pep talk. "I was proud of you today because you worked together like a team. You've all seen how teamwork makes the dream work! Even though you've had a big day, you can't be crabby because the day's not over. When we get out, let's get in a huddle, put our hands together one last time, and on the count of three say, buck up you Buckeyes!"

A postscript to this story... Ohio State won! My son-in-law, Bryan, checked himself into emergency, and was given an IV. Both he and our daughter, Anita, felt better by morning. Later that same evening, we watched the lighted, horse-drawn Christmas parade on Hamilton's Main Street, waved at Santa, and shared pizza and subs at Rose Bros. for supper. Just one final thought. If you ask me, this year's game day quarterback/coach/referee should have been named the Country Cousin's "MVG," Most Valuable Granny.

Ultimate Wish Book

WHILE ON A mini field trip to our town's historic City Hall, the visiting third and fourth graders were mesmerized by the building's adjacent outhouse. Students hesitantly peeked in at the dark little room with a single round hole carved in the wooden bench. As their docent, I informed them, "Toilet paper was probably not used in this or any other outhouse." They wanted to know what was used instead. I told them catalogues were sometimes placed inside for that purpose.

Following a universal groan, a serious voice from the middle of the group asked, "What's a catalogue?" I lamely explained,

"It's similar to a really thick magazine." Barely perceivable nods of understanding indicated this was a "good enough" answer for most, but I was left with the uneasy feeling I hadn't painted an accurate picture. I hadn't given the all-important catalogue the credit it rightly deserved. This was food for thought.

Quite honestly, the student's innocent question caught me off guard. From past teaching experiences, I knew this generation of munchkins was unfamiliar with record players and tape recorders. However, I hadn't realized the catalogue, something so common to our culture a short time ago, had now become something uncommon. For older adults raised in the past century, the catalogue was the most sought- after book in the house. To wise and knowledgeable adults, members of the gray-haired gang, the catalogue was much more than glorified toilet paper. It was your one-stop shopping center.

For kids, it was the book that made all their dreams come true.

There are activities from the past I don't miss like washing dishes by hand, but this child's innocent question gave me a twinge of regret for today's youth. Why? Because they're missing the fun of cozying up on the couch or stretching out on the floor with the best book ever, the Christmas Catalogue. Images filling the pages sparked every kid's imagination and opened up a world of adventure. To eager young dreamers, this thick volume, jam-packed with colorful pictures of toys, held the promise of Christmas wishes fulfilled.

Every November, all across America, kids hurried to their mailbox anticipating the arrival of the J.C. Penney or Sears and Roebuck Christmas Catalogues. When one finally appeared, wrapped in brown paper, curled sideways and stuffed in the mailbox, excitement mounted. Kids eagerly grabbed a pencil and began circling items for Santa's list, marking really important pages with a dog-eared corner. For kids growing up in rural America, the catalogue was their best and sometimes their only connection to the latest fashions and innovations. My husband got his first set of wheels from the Sears and Roebuck catalogue, a motorized bike called a moped, which he still owns.

Today's youth will say their computer serves them just as well as any catalogue. That may be true, but, with a catalogue, you could feel its weight; every ounce full of potential and promise. With a catalogue you could touch the pages first with your fingers, then with your eyes, creating a sensory connection to your imagination; your Christmas wish list of treasures. I feel fortunate to have experienced the anticipation, the excitement, the expectation which accompanied the turn of each thin, smooth page. How special it was to possess the Christmas Catalogue; a giant volume chock-full of hopes, dreams, and wishes that just might come true.

Sneak Peek

AS WE GET older our perspective on Christmas changes, or at least it makes minor adjustments. When I was a kid, the holiday season seemed magical. I remember the days and weeks sandwiched between Thanksgiving and Christmas as special. I'm relieved to say I still embrace all that's magical about the holiday season, but, over the years, something has changed. Back when I was in grade school, I wanted time to speed up, and I don't imagine I was unique in thinking Christmas Day couldn't come fast enough. Now, years later, I wish time would slow down... just a bit, at least.

Why did I want time to speed up? I can summarize it in one word: "presents." It was the allure of certain untouchable "special" presents piled beneath the tree that made time pass at a snail's pace. These presents came by mail, sent early in order to beat the Christmas rush, from my Aunt Leona and Uncle Harry in far-off San Antonio, Texas. There they were, gifts I couldn't open. Gifts in plain sight, but off limits, stacked neatly beneath the decorated Douglas Fir. They were always purchased at Joske's, a Texas Department store chain; professionally wrapped, with large puffy bows made of shiny satin ribbon, just begging to be opened.

Aunt Leona was a no-nonsense person, a farm girl turned school teacher. She married late in life to Uncle Harry, a bookkeeper who had been a Master Sergeant during WWII. Most years the couple sent me the usual practical gifts: splendidly wrapped underpants, socks, and books. Nice gifts, gifts I could use, gifts I appreciated, but nothing I would ever take to school for "Show-and-Tell." This year was different. There was a special present that didn't fit the usual pattern.

I zeroed-in on the box that seemed too small to hold a book and too skinny to be stuffed full of underpants or socks. The temptation was irresistible. So, one night, when my parents were in the kitchen, chatting over coffee, I did the unthinkable. I raised the volume on the TV to cover any noise. Then I quickly loosened the tape, removed the ribbon and paper, opened the lid on the box, and stared at the contents.

Inside was a small book, a joke book. I should have known Aunt Leona and Uncle Harry wouldn't deviate from their plan, wouldn't veer off course. Faster than comedienne Minnie Pearl could say, "Howdy!" I rewrapped the package. I even managed to act surprised when reopening it Christmas morning. Admittedly, some of the jokes came in handy at my classroom's post-Christmas "Show-and-Tell."

As kids go, my son-in-law, Bryan, and I seemed to have a lot in common. Like me, the allure of presents in plain view was hard for him to handle. Again, like me, he set his sights on one particular gift. It was a wrapped box that looked like a video game. Yep! On close inspection it was the right shape, size, and weight. It might even be the one sitting at the very tip-top of his wish list. He made his decision, then waited for his mother to leave for work.

Wow! It was his dream-come-true! For a few seconds he held the Nintendo game in his sweaty hands, wondering what to do next. Knowing his mother would be gone most of the afternoon, he proceeded with the only logical step. He played the video game! Two hours later, after mastering it, he slipped it back into its package. For now,

Sneak Peek

nobody would know. Many years later the truth finally came out.

As a kid I couldn't wait for Christmas to hurry up and get here so I could open my presents. As a senior citizen, I want life to slow down. I want Christmas to take its good old time in getting here, and I definitely don't want or need presents. I've got more than enough stuff!

If you're that person somewhere in the middle, between young and old, I've just given you a priceless Christmas gift. I've allowed you a sneak peek into the future; into the crystal ball where Christmas presents lose their allure, and time becomes more precious than gold.

Pass the Pizza, Please!

During most of mankind's history, the unending search for something to eat consumed every aspect of our ancestors' thoughts, words, and deeds. In the not-so-distant past, a large percentage of a person's life was spent daily hunting and gathering food. Only recently has mankind been able to shop in a grocery store stocked full of staples and treats.

I've had some memorable meal disasters, but they were "No big deal," because nowadays there's always a plan B available in the freezer. What's my plan B, you might ask? I turn to the food everybody else in America turns to when all else fails. My plan B quite simply is pizza.

Yep, pizza has always been my go-to food when a food-flop occurs. There was the time I made a ham. It was my first attempt at preparing a Thanksgiving feast for my dad and boyfriend who later became my husband. I placed the small pink piece of pork in a granite roaster, sprinkled it with juicy pineapple, and turned on the oven to let it cook. The timer buzzed indicating the meat was done, but the three of us weren't ready to eat.

Even with the oven turned off, the ham inside kept right on cooking. Who knew? An hour later I opened the oven and removed the roaster. Surprise! Everything inside had turned into a blackened cinder. The once pink piece of pork transformed into a shriveled-up chunk of charcoal that was permanently cemented to the pan. I had to throw Porky the Pig away with the pot.

Since plan A was a food-flop, I immediately put plan B into action. I went to the freezer, opened a frozen pizza, placed it in the oven, set the timer, and "Voila!" It's always fool proof! Twelve minutes later we had our Thanksgiving feast of pizza with mushrooms and pepperoni.

That same year I prepared our Christmas feast, only this time turkey was my menu's main course. I turned on the oven and placed the turkey inside. Then we waited, and waited, and waited. Six hours later the turkey was still raw. Who knew you shouldn't put a frozen turkey in the oven? The turkey was done around midnight that night. But never fear, plan B was near! This time we had pizza with sausage and mushrooms.

Many years later our whole family gathered for Christmas lunch. Our son, Ryan, and his new bride, Andrea, even brought their dog, Ralph, so he wouldn't be left home alone. Ralph got along just fine with our dog,

Daisy. The two of them kept each other company while we ate.

My turkey and trimmings were a success. We lingered at the table sharing stories while enjoying dessert. Then I wrapped the leftover turkey from the hot roaster in tinfoil and placed it on the dining room table to cool before storing it in the refrigerator. We all took a short walk to burn off some calories.

When we returned to the kitchen, there they were, two partners in crime. Who knew Ralph and Daisy were each part mountain goat? Somehow, they climbed onto the dining room table; I never have figured out how. All the turkey was gone, along with the tinfoil. (In case you're wondering, neither of them got the least bit sick.) I'm convinced they didn't get sick because mountain goats have stomachs of iron.

Well, for supper, you can guess what we had. Since all the turkey was gone, I resorted to my trusty old plan B. We had pizza supreme with leftover stuffing, mashed potatoes, gravy, and green bean casserole on the side.

Eventually I learned from my mistakes. Dogs are now banished to the garage when we go on walks after eating. The ham is removed the minute it's done, and the turkey is always thawed before going into the oven. Consequently, I've had a whole string of flop-free feasts! But never fear. At least three frozen pizzas are neatly tucked away in my freezer, ready to perform their magic at a minute's notice. It's comforting to know there's a backup plan ready and waiting for someone to say, "Pass the pizza, please!"

Canine Conspiracy

SOMETIMES IN JEST I lovingly say, "Our family is going to the dogs." That's because my husband and I, our grown kids, and their spouses have always felt the need to be surrounded by pound puppies. Honestly, our dogs are more than furry friends; they're family.

Forty-some years ago the first place we lived came with a long-haired dachshund named Lady Bug. Please excuse the pun, but this particular house came already "fur"nished. Well, it didn't take long before a mutt, an obvious stray in need of love and attention, showed up on our doorstep. Sparky was a welcome addition, as was Zack,

Amber, and Tubby. This is pretty much the way our life progressed. Some people mark a family event by the date on the back of a picture. Our family marks events by the dogs included in a picture.

From those first early years, fast forward thirty-some years to the Christmas of 2005. At this time my husband and I have three dogs. Two of our children are married and have dogs of their own. The combined total of wagging tails equals eight. That's a whole bunch of happy hounds! It was Christmas, the perfect time for sharing love and joy, even if you're a dog. Here was the plan…

For many years my husband's parents, Ervin and Louise, did their "snowbird" thing by taking off for Texas in the fall and returning to their house across the road in the spring. Every Christmas Eve we routinely passed around the telephone. The temporary Texans always received a heartfelt, "Wish you were here!" from all of us back home in snowy, cold Ohio. That's when I had the bright idea of sending much needed laughter their way in the form of a book. I knew they could use some cheering up around the holidays, because they missed us as much as we missed them.

So, on this particular Christmas, my in-laws received a surprise package in the mail. It was a picture book featuring our dogs: Muffy, Daisy, Ralph, Ollie, Gertie, Hugo, Lula, and Molly. It followed their Christmas escapades throughout my in-law's spotless, unoccupied house in Ohio. The book's story began on Christmas Day with dogs appearing bored after having chewed on their wrapping paper and bows. What this "gang of eight" apparently needed was some "real action," so they unanimously agreed to move their holiday party to that empty house across the road.

Next, we turned the members of the bowser brigade loose, and watched the story unfold. I was ready to capture the mutt mayhem with my trusty disposable camera. The eight dogs had a blast! They chased each other around the house, running up and down the basement steps, hopping on the furniture, rolling on the carpet, and sniffing in every corner. The humans were busy, keeping a watchful eye, just to make sure... well, you know.

When we were about to leave, we couldn't find shy Daisy. In order to escape the rambunctious mob, she hunkered down on the soft cushy bed in the master bedroom and dozed off. The story ended with everyone (dogs and humans) joining Daisy sprawled on the king-sized bed, grinning and saying, "Doggie Biscuits" for the camera. The finished product was a book fourteen pages long with twenty-three photographs accompanied by captions of canine conversations. Our intention was to replace tears of longing with tears of laughter and by all reports, we succeeded.

It's hard to believe so many years have passed since we planned our canine conspiracy and made that book. A lot has changed in our family since then. All eight of the original canine characters are now in doggie heaven. My husband and I no longer depend on dogs to tear up our Christmas bows and paper. That's because our nine grandchildren took over that job. Still, it's comforting to know some things never change. Our family continues to have eight furry friends between us: Chopper, Sweetie Pie, Rocky, Vanna, Tater Tot, Bailer, Hans, and Hazel. This fact simply means I'll continue to lovingly and jokingly say, "Our family is going to the dogs!"

Letter to Santa

Dear Santa,

I HAVE A PROBLEM opening packages, and I sure could use your help. Last week my husband and I were sitting at the kitchen counter drinking coffee. We wanted a snack, so I went to the cupboard for a box of crackers. I opened the box, reached in, and got a single sleeve of saltines. Then I tugged and pulled at the top of the wrapper. Sadly, the crackers remained untouched and uneaten in their cozy container.

Well, Santa, after my failed attempt to open the crackers, my husband said, "Hand them over. I'll open them." So I passed the still-sealed packet to my "better half." He also tried to tear the top off the wrapper. No luck! Then he did what he always does when all else fails. He used his teeth. I said what I always say when he uses his central incisors instead of scissors, "Don't do that! Remember how you chipped your front tooth biting on a fishing line?"

We couldn't believe it, Santa. After all that work, we still had an unopened pack of buttery, lightly salted saltines in front of us. Both of us had tried, and both of us failed to simply tear open the package. It's true we're getting older, and our strength isn't what it used to be, but give me a break; a cracker wrapper isn't Fort Knox.

In desperation we decided our struggle to penetrate the package wasn't our fault. The manufacturer must have accidentally sealed the top of the wrapper with Gorilla Glue. I asked my husband if he wanted to try a chain saw or a pair of scissors next. The frustration on his face said chain saw, but his voice said, "Scissors will be fine..." Together, we finally sat crunching on the crackers in deflated silence.

I've observed my inability to open packages isn't limited to wrapped crackers. Christmas is close, so I hope you don't mind, Santa, but last week I bought each of my four older grandchildren a small toy. I soon discovered even scissors couldn't cut through the thick, outer plastic container. I wondered what it would take to successfully open these packages. Would I need to use an axe, a crowbar, or even dynamite? With four squirming bodies gathered around and eight eager eyes focused on their unopened presents, the pressure was more than I could handle.

Not wanting them to see their grandma fail attempting to open such small packages, I herded them into the living room. Then I put in the DVD "Frozen," gave them popcorn, and ordered them to watch the movie. Having relocated my audience, I now felt ready to tackle the toys. Since scissors hadn't worked, I opened the knife drawer. Which one would work best: the small steak knife or the large butcher knife? I decided smaller was better and began stabbing and jabbing at the stiff impenetrable plastic.

The plastic pieces were razor sharp, but I was determined not to let a few minor cuts stop me. A quick trip to the medicine cabinet and I was as good as new. After all, I was a grandma on a mission, and my mission wasn't finished. On the inside of the package each toy was fastened to a solid piece of cardboard with wire twist ties and thick straps. I dug through my tool box, located my trusty wire cutters, and sang, "Let it go, let it go!" along with the movie as I snipped at the bonds holding the toys in place. It was truly a Christmas miracle that by the end of the movie I had triumphantly freed all four toys from their package prison. More importantly, in the eyes of the Country Cousins, my "granny with grit" status was still intact.

Cellophane packaging can also present a challenge. Last week I bought a CD of Christmas carols. I wanted to hear songs while driving home, so I needed to open the package. First, I tried to find a place where I could tear off the see-through wrapper, but couldn't find a single seam or glued edge. There was no place where I could grip onto the cellophane. Without a toolbox in my car, I used the only thing I could think of. Holding my car keys in one hand, I scraped the rough, metal edge across the plastic wrapper. Eventually I tore through the clear film, but I also cracked the CD's plastic container.

Santa, I have one more package problem to share. Once I manage to get the "child proof" cap off an aspirin bottle, I still can't get to the aspirin tablets. That's because of the super-duper, incredibly strong paper they've glued across the opening. Since my arthritic thumbs can't punch through that stuff, I have to stab at it with a pencil or ice pick.

From one senior citizen to another, I'm asking you for a great big favor. Please get your elves to make packages easier for us grandmas and grandpas to open. That's really all I want for Christmas. If you can do this, I promise I'll have a giant box of frosted sugar cookies, a thermos full of hot chocolate, and a bag of reindeer treats waiting by the fireplace for you on Christmas Eve. I promise to make sure you'll be able to open all three before heading back to your sleigh. Thanks for making the world a brighter place.

Your loyal admirer,

Konnie Lee Meyer

P.S. If Christmas Eve turns out to be a particularly cold night, feel free to take any one of the blanket throws on the back of our couch. None are handmade heirlooms. I buy my blankets at Dollar General.

Hide-and-Seek

MANY YEARS HAVE passed since I played hide-and-seek with my children. I'm not talking about the game where one person tries to find those who are hiding. I'm talking about the hide-and-seek of Christmas presents. That's the game where all children magically transform into Indiana Jones, the explorer. The object of this game is to secretly search through every nook and cranny, every closet and attic, every basement and shed for Christmas gifts parents have hidden away.

Sometimes parents are successful, and the presents remain undiscovered. If kids do find that special hiding spot, their parents will be the last to know. They'll remain clueless for years. After all, kids don't want to blow their cover. They'll rarely admit to getting an "up close and personal" look at their soon-to-be Christmas presents.

Our oldest son, Ryan, now a grown man, a farmer and a father of three, recently confessed to conducting his own successful seek-and-search mission. In his words, he found the holy grail, "The best gift ever!" Squirreled away in an upstairs closet, wedged among other gifts, was a big, yellow, remote control airplane. Following his discovery, he spent sleepless nights tossing and turning, dreaming of Christmas morning and the time he would take his plane outside for its maiden flight.

Christmas morning came and went. All the presents were unwrapped, but there was no remote control plane. What happened? Where was it? Had the plane been a figment of his imagination? Was it all just a dream?

Hide-and-Seek

Flooded with disappointment, he knew he couldn't ask about it. He couldn't let his parents know he had scouted out the presents. For years he wondered in silence, "What exactly had gone wrong?"

Decades later he discovered the truth, and the answer was simple. I had buyer's remorse. The plane had complicated controls, and I decided he was too young to fly it by himself. Unaware of his discovery, I returned it to the store for a refund. If I'd known how much he wanted that plane, I may have reconsidered. Some stories take a while to have a happy ending. Three decades later he got the toy of his dreams, a drone he uses to inspect his crops. For me, there's one small upside to this story. I didn't have to pay for either plane.

Most kids can't wait to open presents. It's human nature. If you're a parent, don't be fooled. Before the big day, your kids are searching high and low, looking for that secret hiding place where all the Christmas goodies are stashed. Here's wishing parents good luck with your annual game of Christmas hide-and-seek. Years later you'll find out if you were successful... or not! "Ho, Ho, Ho!"

Evening in Paris

I'M MAKING A Christmas wish list. My list progresses from most likely to receive to practically no chance of ever getting. At the top of my list is perfume. At the bottom is a car. While making this list I thought about the variety of product names on both the top and bottom. Have you ever wondered who thinks up the names for all these things? Is there actually a job in which a person is hired to be the corporate name-thinker-upper?

The job description for this person must be to, "Open a dictionary. Run your index finger down the rows of words. Then shout, 'Eureka!' when the perfect word is found; the one that conjures up the desired image."

Words such as Venture, Intrepid, and Mustang are a few of the image-forming names given to cars. These words speak of speed, power, distance, and the open road. Nobody would name a car Penguin, Begonia, or Twinkle. Words such as these evoke the wrong image.

I've noticed a similar approach in naming perfumes. My very first encounter with a "store-bought" fragrance came at a Murphy's Five and Dime Store. I was around six years old when I spotted the exotic-sounding Evening in Paris perfume. It wasn't the bottle or its contents that got my attention. It was the name. What girl wouldn't want to spend an evening in Paris? Even to a six-year-old it sounded like a whole lot of fun. I pictured Cinderella in her beautiful gown, going to the ball to meet the prince of her dreams... in Paris, no less. I'm pretty sure I didn't know where Paris was, but that didn't matter.

This fragrance became my mother's Christmas gift for the next few years. If it had been named "Afternoon in Toledo," would I still have bought it for my mom? Somehow, I doubt it. Poor Mom! Years later I discovered my sister, when she was little, got her the same perfume for Christmas. (I wouldn't be surprised if our brother had too.) Mom probably had enough Evening in Paris bottles stashed away to start her own perfume store.

When I was in high school there were fragrances that targeted teenage buyers. Television commercials and magazine ads told girls they should buy Wind Song because, "Wind Song stays on your mind." Sometimes I wore Heaven Scent. One of my friends always wore Tabu. After those teenage years, I never stuck to one particular fragrance.

Sometimes I'd get perfume as a gift. I'd wear it until it was gone, and that would be the end of that. Then one day, a few years ago, I decided to select a scent. My mother-in-law, Louise, liked one called White

Shoulders. I remembered my Aunt Leona wearing Chanel #5. I was a school teacher in my late fifties. The way I figured it, "It was high time I picked a perfume and stuck to it!"

My search for a scent led me to a local store where I stood staring at shelves full of bottles. There were all those names; names that sounded enticing but were unfamiliar. There were names like Passion, Obsession, and Promise. More confused than ever, I doubted if I could ever narrow it down to make a choice. Then my eyes landed on a familiar label. It was Tabu, the perfume my friend wore in high school. I remembered it as a pleasant fragrance, so I bought it. Finally, I was committed to wearing one particular brand of perfume.

The following day, getting ready for work was the usual routine with one exception. Before I walked out the door, I gave myself a good dose of Tabu, then drove to my job as a third grade teacher. That year there

Evening in Paris

was one little girl who came into my room before other students. As usual, she plopped her books on her desk, and handed me her homework. While scrunching up her nose and pointing it in the air, she sniffed deeply three times, then asked, "EEW, what smells?"

"That would be me! I'm trying a new perfume." There was silence. Next, I hopefully inquired, "Do you like it?" With the honesty of a child she replied, "Well, you smell just like my great grandmother. She's 98. She's in a nursing home. My mom and I visit her there every week. Yep, you smell just like her and the nursing home!"

I felt deflated. This wasn't the response I was aiming for. After complimenting the little girl for visiting her great grandmother, I made a mental note to try a different fragrance (which I still have not done).

Like I said, perfume is at the top of my Santa list, and just about any old bottle of perfume will do (I'll say "yes" to pretty much everything except, Tabu). A car is at the bottom of my list, and a magazine picture of an old Ford Mustang will likewise do just fine. Scratch that! It's almost Christmas, so let me be honest. What I'd really like to do is spend an evening in Paris with my husband zooming around in a brand-new Ferrari. Hey! A girl can always dream!

Real Deal

IF YOU'RE A kid at Christmas, finding the real Santa seems like an impossible task. During the month of December, everywhere you look, there are white-bearded men dressed in fuzzy, red outfits, each trying to look and act like that original jolly old elf.

As a parent and true believer, I explained to my three children at an early age, "These guys aren't the real Santa. They're simply dressed like him. They're hired to play the part because the authentic one, the real one, is busy working overtime at the North Pole."

Honestly, most kids above the age of four can't be fooled because they are observation experts. For example, they know the real

Santa doesn't have bits of black neck hair peeking out beneath a white wig. They know the real Santa isn't skinny. He doesn't have a pointy nose, or brown, pointy shoes tied with shoelaces, and he would never dream of wearing high-water pants. Santa doesn't have a scraggly beard inching below his mouth when he talks, and the real Mr. Claus doesn't have breath that hints of tobacco.

The bona fide Santa is more mysterious, and more magical than any of today's common imposters. Close your eyes and imagine the true Santa in your mind, the one from your childhood. Your genuine Santa has sparkly, clear-blue eyes, wears white gloves, and has wire rimmed spectacles perched on the end of his round, red nose. His soft, luxurious suit covers his ample belly, and his curly white beard and mustache are equally thick and fluffy. His voice and appearance are more wonderful than all of the commercial interpretations of him. My fear is that Santa's mystique decreases each time we expose our children to these fake facsimiles.

When our oldest child, Ryan, was three, I made an error in judgment by signing the two of us up for what was billed as, "Breakfast with Santa." I thought it might be fun. In my head I pictured Santa strolling in, lightly patting each child on the head, while saying in a deep resounding voice, "Always be sure to eat breakfast, boys and girls. It's the most important meal of the day!" Then he would wave good-bye and exit.

In reality, the whole thing was a flop, a fiasco. All the kids sat with their parents at a long table. In walked the so-called guest of honor. He must have been famished, because, without a single "HO, HO, HO!" he plopped down, lifted his beard with one hand while shoveling scrambled eggs into his mouth with the other. My son looked up at me with a puzzled expression. I winked and said, "This guy doesn't have very good table manners. He should have at least put the napkin on his lap." Then I whispered, "He's not the real Santa."

Eventually, around third grade, our son became suspicious of Santa's authenticity. I could tell, for the sake of his younger sister, Anita, he was playing along with the pretense. I knew his more "Santa savvy" classmates had been filling his mind with secrets. They had been giving him the scoop on Saint Nick, causing him to teeter on the brink of becoming a bah-humbug boy. It broke my heart. He was too young to become a Santa skeptic.

Through the grapevine I heard the "real Santa" was coming to a mall in the nearby big city of Toledo. Talk about perfect timing! As our two kids stood in line, their eyes zeroed in on the big guy in red. An imposing figure, this Santa looked as though he could easily handle a sleigh, eight prancing reindeer, and a giant bag of toys. Beside his chair rested a gnarled wooden staff. He was a burly guy with a booming voice to match. He passed the initial visual and auditory inspection with flying colors.

What happened next made us all lifetime believers. When our "doubting Thomas" son approached, Santa said, "I remember you. You're the boy who lives in the two-story white house with black shutters." My husband and I looked at each other and shrugged. Awe struck, our son could only nod in the affirmative. To this day, our family talks about that once-in-a-lifetime close encounter with the real deal.

Recently our grandson, Bo sat through a photo session with Santa. On the ride home he shocked his parents by declaring, "I don't ever want Santa to come to my house!" Puzzled, Ali and Rob reminded him, "Santa's the guy who brings presents at Christmas." Bo was silent.

"Don't you want Santa to deliver your toys?" they asked. His reply made sense. "No! I don't want any toys from him! He told me I had to be a good boy. I can't be a good boy all the time, so I don't want him to come to my house." They quickly reassured him Santa just wants boys and girls to "try" to be good.

Each December, a handful of my "growing doubtful" third grade students quizzed me about the "big guy." They asked me if I believed in him. My answer was always the same. "Of course I believe in Santa! I know he's real! He lives and works at the North Pole. He remains forever in the hearts and minds of all who believe."

Potluck Panic

WHENEVER AND WHEREVER groups of people gather, food is naturally involved. Reunions, weddings, birthdays, meetings, team tributes, and church functions all call for a large feast of one kind or another. But none of these dining delights compares to what comes in November and December. Most Americans would agree that the longest-lasting food-feasting season of them all are the days between Thanksgiving and Christmas. During this particular time of year, we get to sample and savor all sorts of culinary delights. My salivary glands activate, and my mouth begins to water just dreaming about holiday feasts.

Every workplace and organization celebrates the holidays in its own way. Office workers bring in cookies. Volunteers contribute baskets of candy which are set on counters for everyone to enjoy. Hot chocolate, eggnog, or spiced cider may be added to the familiar routine of a coffee break. Everywhere you turn, there's the temptation to take and taste.

In many parts of our country the most popular of all food feasts is the potluck. At potluck dinners, second and third helpings are welcomed. At potluck dinners, you aren't responsible for buying and cooking all the food; you're only responsible for one item. At a potluck, the variety of food seems endless. It appears to be the perfect way to throw a holiday party... or is it?

Being a retired teacher, I can attest to the fact that school employees are big potluck participants. They embrace the festive, or should I say, "feastive" season just like everyone else. I do miss the kids and their eager anticipation of the holidays. I do miss my colleagues and their commitment to educating those same kids who are wound up, hyper, and bouncing off the walls during all the holiday hoopla. Call me the Grinch, but if I'm to be totally honest, I don't miss those staff potluck meals.

Oh sure, like everyone else, I looked forward to the aroma of simmering delicacies drifting down the hallways. But here's the thing. What always put me in a panic was deciding which dish to bring. If I made something common, I feared nobody would eat it. Who wants to be the only one to cart home a filled-to-the-brim crockpot full of crusty mac-and-cheese? That can be humiliating. If I made something really fancy, my family would say, "Why don't you ever make something good like that for us?" What's a gal to do? It's a dietary dilemma that can easily morph into a pressure cooker of a food fiasco.

Oh, and one more thing. There's my fear of forgetting to bring my culinary contribution to the preplanned potluck on the designated day. In my defense, "It's a busy time of the year!" But I learned the hard way; forgetting your delicious dish at home, not doing your part, failing to keep the potluck promise, is not considered kosher. Your name could be banned or placed on a black-list, with your punishment being to never-ever participate in future potluck parties. (Punishment or reward, I ask?)

This happened to my son-in-law, Rob, who at the time was a teacher when he signed up for the staff potluck. He volunteered to bring those ever-popular nachos with all the trimmings. His only mistake was, he failed to inform Ali, his wife, which is how most men deal with their potluck cooking obligations. This meant no loaded nachos for this group. Not wanting to arrive empty-handed, he made a quick morning sprint to the nearby gas station, grabbing pop and plastic cups. This wasn't exactly nachos and dip, but the way he figured it, both items could be stored indefinitely and used at a later date. Quick thinking preserved his seat at the potluck party.

Some Christmas potluck planners insist on getting creative. They attempt to amplify holiday festivities by giving the party a theme. The theme could be a dessert bar, salad bar, or a tail-gate picnic. At any rate, theme potlucks did very little to relieve my stress levels. I'm first to admit that my kitchen culinary skills are limited. I make meat and potatoes or soup and sandwich; nothing fancy; nothing out of the ordinary. So, whenever I heard whispers of a themed potluck, I made sure I got to the sign-up sheet before the guys. That way I could be first to volunteer for the sure-fire stand-by... a bag of potato chips. Chips fit with any theme, dessert included. I love potato chips! Lay's Wavy original are the best! I've been known to eat them for dessert instead of pie. Besides, left-over chips never go to waste. They make a great after-school snack.

Despite all my misgivings, I do realize the many positives of hosting a potluck party. Consequently, here's a holiday heads-up to my kids. From this point forward, on every Thanksgiving and Christmas, it's potluck all the way. You're all responsible for divvying up the yummy dishes. No themes and no sign-up sheets. I'll supply the plates, silverware, drinks, and potato chips. That's your mom's holiday potluck pledge, and I'm sticking to it!

Table-time

THERE ARE MANY American traditions once common to everyday life that have vanished or become obsolete. Spending quality time around a table is one such tradition. Not so long ago, families sat at a table enjoying, at the very least, one home cooked meal a day. In today's fast-paced society, families often order their meal at a drive-through window; eating in the car. The gradual disappearance of family table-time may be a topic worth closer examination.

In years past, sitting together as a family, at a table, to eat the evening meal, happened as a matter of unquestioning routine. In households everywhere this occurred without interruption and without exception. It was the one time during each day when all family members were expected to unite in body and spirit to share fellowship and food.

Twenty-first century families face hectic schedules, causing members to eat "on-the-run," and nibble "on-the-go." Who hasn't heard someone say while hurrying out the door, "I'll catch a bite later!" With both parents working and children involved with after-school lessons and extracurricular activities, there's little chance for all family members to sit and eat at a common time or place. The evening mealtime has morphed into a rushed affair. It's now something that happens individually or in partial family groups, but modern suppertime rarely includes the entire family unit, sitting together around a table.

Changes in this once steadfast tradition may not at first glance seem all that important, but in my opinion it has far-reaching, society- changing consequences.

Table-time

Let's examine. Besides food consumption, what was so positive about everyone sitting together around a table? What have we lost by not continuing to observe this time-honored tradition?

Back in the day, most evening meals began by reciting a common table prayer in unison. Repeating this prayer with heads bowed and hands folded, taught children the importance of being thankful for God's gifts. It was a basic but meaningful life lesson in being humble and grateful for things we might otherwise take for granted.

When families gathered together for an evening meal, the children learned responsibility, leadership, and time management skills. It was the younger members who set the table, making sure everyone had a plate, napkin, silverware, and glass. Concentration and steady hands were needed for older children to safely transfer food from the stove to the table. With so much effort going into a meal, there was no excuse for showing up late to the table.

Conversation around the table led to a broadening of vocabulary, as well as the sharing of opinions and family values. Congenial discussions and debates helped children fine-tune their logic, mediation, and thinking skills. When describing participation in daily activities, family members gained a sense of accomplishment and pride.

Sitting at a table as a family unit also gave parents a chance to teach their children important table manners. Chew with your mouth closed. When passing food, say "please and thank you," and don't ever talk with your mouth full. Put your napkin on your lap while eating, and when you're finished, rest it beside your plate. Don't leave the table until "you're excused."

Following a meal, dirty dishes, bowls, and utensils had to be removed, scraped, and added to the sink full of soapy, hot water.

Table-time

Before automatic dishwashers, the eating event ended only after everybody pitched in with washing, drying, and putting items back on shelves. Children quickly learned about teamwork, because with everyone helping, the individual workload was lessened.

With Christmas just around the corner, there will hopefully be many opportunities for families to spend time not just sitting and eating but talking and sharing stories while gathered around a table. It seems like such a simple and perhaps insignificant tradition, but looking back, it's the source of some of my most endearing and enduring memories. This Christmas, make room in those busy schedules for some additional table-time. It just might be one of the most meaningful gifts parents can give their children.

Silent Night

CHRISTMAS IS MOST certainly a top contender for busiest season of the year. In our already hectic schedules, we may feel additional pressure to carve out time to do multiple activities. I'm guilty of being caught up in the Christmas frenzy as much as the next person. Therefore, I feel qualified to give a sampling of what Christmas has become for most Americans, myself included.

We feel obligated to scour store shelves and the internet in search of perfect gifts. After finding and purchasing these gifts, we wrap them with paper and ribbon, or conceal them in special bags. We spend hours cooking and baking holiday foods and treats;

annual favorites to share with family and friends. We send stacks of cards to loved ones near and far. But wait, that's not all.

We shuttle kids to various practices and spend evenings helping them memorize parts. Then, we shop for their clothes or costumes to be worn at their performances. We devote time to stringing lights and decorating trees, both inside and outside. We help little ones write their Christmas wish lists and once completed, we take these hopeful cherubs to meet that "jolly old elf" in person. Some of us must then pack suitcases and travel hundreds of miles to be with loved ones. So, how can we manage to stay calm during the holidays when faced with a "to do" list a mile long?

I'm no expert, but I have a suggestion that works for me. When frazzled by all the frantic festivities, I think of that very first Christmas over two-thousand years ago. Using words written by Joseph Mohr in the

Silent Night

Austrian hymn, it was on this special "Silent Night" a baby was born in humble surroundings. There was no glitz or glam. There was no shiny tinsel on twinkling trees. Nope! There were two young, soon-to-be parents whose faith brought them to this unlikely place of birth. On this particular night, like the hymn says, "All is calm."

Sometimes I try, but I honestly can't imagine how difficult this first Christmas must have been for the parents involved. Poor Mary! She had to have been extremely tired, scared, and uncomfortable! Ready to give birth at any moment, she bravely rode miles over rough terrain on the back of a donkey to their ancestral home of Bethlehem. I'm sure all she really wanted was to get off that animal and find a nice, quiet, comfortable place to rest.

Poor Joseph as well! Following the journey, he surely was concerned for his expectant wife. He too must have been exhausted from walking the entire distance leading the donkey. After searching throughout the town for a place to stay, he probably felt discouraged to find all rooms occupied. Most likely he was relieved to at least locate a stable. This outdoor shed full of animals was better than nothing at all.

Despite these difficulties, their healthy baby boy was born! I'm certain Mary and Joseph's hearts were bursting with joy. But, I also wonder if their minds weren't somewhat burdened after hearing from an angel about their son's future role as Jesus, our Lord and Savior. I'm guessing they knew from Biblical prophecy exactly what that meant. That's a lot for two young parents to absorb.

Every time I hear the hymn "Silent Night," my eyes fill with tears, and I'm not sure why. Perhaps the song reminds me of the basic simplicity of that first Christmas so many years ago. Perhaps it's because I know what lies ahead for that tiny babe in the manger and am grateful for his willing sacrifice. Perhaps I'm nostalgic about sitting on my mother's lap, listening to this hymn being sung in church. Could it be this song helps me think of what's truly important in life: faith and family? Maybe I get teary eyed because of all the above.

Like I said, I'm not an expert, but when you feel overwhelmed with the hustle and bustle of baking, shopping, wrapping, decorating, and planning... just stop! Take a minute to focus and reflect on that first Christmas when there was a mother, a father, and the miracle of their newborn son. Without this special "Silent Night," there would be no Christmas! Now, doesn't that truly make everything else seem a whole lot less important?

Holiday Superheroes

IF YOU'RE THE director of a performing group, Christmastime is when you become a superhero. All across America, this is the season when children and adults repeatedly gather to rehearse for their annual holiday performance. Spearheading a holiday pageant or choral musical event takes hours of preparation. It takes a boatload of organizational skills. It requires tons of patience, and, in my humble opinion, it takes a will of iron and nerves of steel.

Group leadership also takes a certain amount of flexibility, which means being prepared to expect the unexpected. This is especially true when dealing with children.

They're unpredictable. Simply getting them to form a straight line and stand still on stage can be as frustrating as herding cats. Because their attention span is limited, even if you're lucky enough to have gotten them where they should be, there's no guarantee they'll stay there. With kids, you're never quite certain what will happen next.

Think back to past Christmas performances you've observed. There is always one child who belts out, "Hi, Mom!" while waving vigorously to the crowd. There's always one child that sings way off key with gusto, much louder than all the others combined. There's always one who misses their cue, staring blankly at the audience while failing to speak their part. There's always one who can't stand still (needing to use the restroom) and proceeds to dance an unchoreographed jig on stage. There's always one who stands yawning, due to a delayed bedtime or missed nap. Occasionally, there's one who gets stage fright and cries, resulting in removal from the group.

There can be a variety of unpredictable mishaps, catching both the director and the audience off guard. When my son-in-law, Rob, was six, he had to fill in for an absent, older performer. His new assignment was to "be a Christmas present." With the help of an adult, he slipped his head and arms through the oversized, cardboard box which was decorated to look like a wrapped gift.

All this happened during his "cowboy boot" phase of childhood. Everywhere he went he wore his cowboy boots, and this special performance was no exception. As he stomped across the stage wearing his ill-fitted costume and clunky boots, he accidentally tripped, falling backward, leaving the surprised audience to see only legs and boots flailing in the air. To say the least, his performance made a lasting impression.

Many years ago, I attended a choral performance in which singers were standing on risers. The room was exceedingly warm, making the situation difficult for those in the spotlight. In the middle of a song, the audience was startled to hear a persistent, low moan overpowering the music. Puzzled, the audience began looking at one another for answers.

For a while the singing and groaning continued, but as the unidentified, eerie sound grew in intensity, the director, realizing something was wrong, silenced the singers. Only then was it discovered one of the overheated back row singers had passed out, quietly sinking to the floor unnoticed. Fortunately, or perhaps unfortunately, the person's mouth ended up inches away from the sound system, amplifying the mournful moans throughout the room. You've heard the saying, "The show must go on." After a brief period, the singer, a real trooper, recovered, and the Christmas tribute continued.

Whenever costumes are involved, it's a sure bet there will be wardrobe malfunctions. Reindeer can have antler problems, angels can have wing problems, and that jolly old elf, Santa, can have problems too numerous to mention. During my third grade class reenactment of "The Polar Express," Santa's pants began to droop until eventually they ended up around his knees. With a firm grip on his bothersome britches, Santa hiked them up. Weaving his way between stunned elves and reindeer, he walked off stage, found his mom in the audience, had her tighten the drawstring, then calmly returned to the spotlight where he proceeded to flawlessly fulfill his duties as Santa.

Nowadays Christmas program directors must deal with issues that didn't exist just a few years ago. Past directors didn't have to mess with complicated sound systems.

They never had to ask audiences to silence their phones, and they didn't have to cope with guests leaving their seats to take pictures or videos. Today kids are involved in a multitude of activities, so just scheduling a common time to rehearse can become a director's worst nightmare.

Christmas is a magical time of the year. We're fortunate to have dedicated people willing to work at making holiday programs and Christmas pageants special events to be remembered. This and every year let's not forget to show our gratitude and appreciation to those talented superheroes who help spread joy and the Christmas message.

Miraculous Scotch Tape

I SOMETIMES THINK, AS a society; we've become so blasé, so out of touch with our surroundings, that it's easy to overlook miracles. I'm convinced miracles are everywhere. You just need to know what to look for. It's a matter of perspective. Push a button and our dishes are clean. Push another button and our food cooks within seconds. Turn on a switch and darkness disappears. Not so long ago all of this would have been unimaginable fiction.

It's oh so easy to take common items for granted. We don't often see them as the wonderful miracles they are. Think how difficult our lives would be in the absence of everyday items like canned food, hand soap, toilet paper, and ink pens. We've come to depend on such things; things we can't do without. Perhaps the fact we have them at all is a miracle. For the purpose of this story, my focus is on one seemingly insignificant, yet miraculous item: Scotch tape.

Good old Scotch tape has come to my rescue many times. Once, while teaching, the hem of my skirt caught on a chair, causing the stitching to completely unravel. Scotch tape to the rescue! On another occasion, a flight to Texas that should have taken five hours, due to bad weather, took twelve hours instead. Fortunately, I had stuffed four rolls of Scotch tape into my diaper bag to entertain our two-year-old daughter, Anita. Scotch tape was everywhere: on the window, the seat, the ceiling, even the fold-out tray. Putting on, pulling off, and wadding up tape kept our daughter entertained for hours. I'd call that a minor miracle.

Miraculous Scotch Tape

The ultimate Scotch tape miracle happened a few years ago on Christmas Eve. This story involves our son, Ryan, Andrea his wife, Gus their three-year-old, and Evie their eighteen-month-old toddler. When the family arrived at church, they were greeted by an Elder. He needed volunteers to light the advent candle and place the baby Jesus doll in the manger in front, by the altar. The tasks sounded simple, so the parents agreed to help.

Juggling two small children, a heavy diaper bag, a baby doll and a Bic lighter, they struggled down the aisle. After finding their seats, and reading the church bulletin, they discovered their jobs came at the end of the service. Bummer! This meant they had to stay for the entire Christmas Eve program, which also meant, if the service lasted too long and their two kiddos got antsy or rambunctious, they couldn't silently sneak out to the car.

At first everything went smoothly, but halfway into the program things started to deteriorate. The battle of the babies began. The two real babies each claimed possession of the fake one. The doll was old and brittle. Frankly, it had "seen better days." A game of "don't-touch-the-doll" ensued. The parents stuffed the doll in the diaper bag. That didn't work. They hid it under the pew. Nope, the kiddos found it. They covered it with their coats. Same result. To both parents this felt like the longest Christmas Eve Service on record. Then the unthinkable happened!

While shuffling the doll from one place to another, it tumbled to the floor. The doll's body shot under the pew in front, while the head rolled back two pews. Now what? They couldn't put a headless doll in the manger. Andrea frantically scooped up the pieces and rushed to seek help from the Elders. While showing them what happened, the doll accidentally slipped from her hands, causing an arm to break off! She said a silent prayer.

Miraculous Scotch Tape

Taking too long to set, glue was not an option. What she needed was a miracle, and the sooner the better. An Elder checked the office with no luck. Andrea searched the classrooms. Eureka! Finding a full roll of Scotch tape, she quickly wrapped the doll's separated parts with yards and yards of the sticky stuff. It didn't look pretty, but it worked. It held!

In the nick of time, cradling the mini miracle in her arms, Andrea hurried down the aisle, pausing briefly beside her pew to gather her family. While holding his son, Ryan lit the advent candle. Andrea and Evie placed the bedraggled and bandaged doll in the manger. It was a second minor miracle Evie didn't have a melt-down while surrendering baby Jesus. Perhaps she thought the doll now looked too strange with all those strings of Scotch tape holding it together.

I truly believe in major and minor miracles. They happen all the time. We're surrounded by them. But we must be willing to search for them and recognize them in our everyday lives. Maybe we simply need to keep an open mind and a believing heart. Oh, it might not hurt to keep a roll of Scotch tape close by too.

Savor the Season

THIS IS NOT one of our family's Christmas stories, but it's a story worth sharing. As we frantically hustle from store to store in search of the perfect gifts, it's inevitable our level of stress rises like the mercury in a thermometer on a hot summer's day. Tight budgets, time limitations, crowded stores, and packed parking lots add up to make gift-giving a bit overwhelming. It sometimes happens that, in our quest for the perfect presents, we risk losing sight of the true meaning and spirit of Christmas.

I have a gift I want to give to you, my readers. It's a simple Christmas story that has been told and retold through the ages.

I hope it will help to ease your panic over presents. But before you read any further, take a minute to unwind. It's important to savor the season. Go ahead and make yourself some hot chocolate, mulled cider, or eggnog. Then kick back, relax, and sip away as you read, **"The Legend of the Poinsettia."**

Once upon a time there was a young girl named Maria. She had a little brother whom she loved dearly named Pablo. The two children were very poor, but they were happy because they had each other. Every year they looked forward to the Christmas festival held in their small Mexican village. The celebration lasted for days and was filled with colorful parades, bright lights, and music.

During this time, for as long as anyone could remember, it had also been a custom in their village to set up a large manger scene inside the local church. On Christmas Eve, the people of the village and the surrounding countryside brought gifts to be placed in the manger which held Baby Jesus. Maria and Pablo eagerly awaited Christmas and all the festivities it brought, but each year they were saddened because they had no money to buy presents. Most of all they longed to buy a gift for that tiny baby wrapped in a blanket lying in the manger.

One Christmas Eve the two children set out for church. They were worried this year would be the same as all the others, and they would once again arrive at the church with nothing to give. Along the way they rested, comforted by their determination to find something they could bring. Both children agreed they too would show their love for the tiny baby by presenting him with a gift, any gift, no matter how small. As they continued on, they noticed tall weeds growing beside the road, and they bent down to pick them. They each tightly grasped a bundle of the green, spindly plants, satisfied this would be the gift they'd give to the tiny newborn.

By the time they arrived at church, the manger was overflowing with beautiful presents, and their fistful of weeds hung limp and drooping in their little hands. The other children and adults of the village taunted and teased Maria and Pablo when they appeared with their bedraggled bundles. Everyone laughed at the thought of bringing weeds to church as a present for the Christ Child, and they told the two children that theirs was an unfit gift for such a special baby. Maria and Pablo ignored the voices and remained silent, for they knew they had given what they could and had nothing else to offer. As the villagers looked on, they watched the two children carefully separate each plant from the bundle and tenderly place the weeds around the manger.

When Maria and Pablo finished, they stood back staring in awe and amazement as the green leaves of the weeds miraculously sprouted into large, brilliant, red petals.

Before long the entire manger was a sea of crimson, surrounded by the beautiful star-like flowers of the poinsettia.

I hope you enjoyed the story and will consider sharing it with a friend or loved one. During all the hustle and bustle of Christmas we might want to slow down, take a deep breath, and remember it's not about the shopping, decorations, wrapping, or finding those perfect presents. Christmas is about the baby in the manger and the true spirit in which a gift is given.

Go ahead! Pour yourself another round of hot chocolate, mulled cider or eggnog. On second thought, like Country Cousins, Mack, Gus, Evie, Meyta, Cece, Bo, Malone, and Larkin (by next Christmas, baby Ike too) often do - you could politely ask someone (it's usually their Pawpaw) to stir up an old-fashioned, frothy root-beer float. Sounds refreshing, doesn't it? Whatever beverage you choose, it's important to remember... take time to savor the season.

Christmas Correspondence

How many letters have you written lately? My guess is few or none-at-all. Letter writing has become obsolete, a thing of the past, a lost art. Granted, it's time-consuming. Besides, if a person wants to communicate in writing, there now are many options. People have computers and cell phones. We can e-mail, text message, or tweet. Who needs paper and pencil?

Some of you may remember the old Pat Boone song about writing "Love Letters in the Sand." That song makes no sense today. It seems far-fetched for someone to sing about a scratched love note on the beach. In order to relate to modern teens, the lyrics would have to be rewritten to describe typing "emojis on a screen."

Singer and television host Perry Como used to have a segment on his weekly show in which he answered fan mail. He'd reach his hand into a giant barrel filled with hundreds of letters, while singing, "Letters, we get letters. We get stacks and stacks of letters." Then he'd grab one, open it, and read it to his audience. After answering questions contained in the letter, he'd then sing the particular song request. Wow! Forget about the songs! I wanted to get stacks of letters just like Perry Como!

So, during one summer vacation I began a letter writing campaign. The way I figured it, in order to get lots of letters, I had to write lots of letters. My strategy was to write to movie stars. I got their addresses from the back pages of teen magazines. In each letter

Christmas Correspondence

I requested an autographed picture. Then all I had to do was sit back and wait for the mail to come pouring in.

Each day, when the mailman came, I raced to the mailbox. Lawrence Welk took the prize, being first to reply. He not only sent me an autographed picture, but he included a two-page handwritten letter thanking me for being a fan of the "Champaign Music Makers." Imagine my shock when I also got a signed Christmas card from him that year. He sent a card for many years after that. What a guy! I wasn't sure if he didn't get much fan mail, or he was just that nice. I think it was the latter.

To this day I feel kind of guilty about the whole thing. I didn't intentionally try to mislead Mr. "Wonerful, Wonerful," but I really wasn't what you'd call a huge fan. I preferred the rock and roll records my older brother played. I just wanted to get letters in the mail. After all, I was pursuing my hobby, and Mr.

Welk's address just happened to be included in the movie star magazine.

Mr. Welk, or should I say Lawrence, since we were on a first-name, Christmas-card basis, entered my family's living room every weekend for years. There was only one small black and white television in the house, so that meant if my parents watched the champaign bubbles float across the screen, I watched them too. I had no choice.

The Lennon Sisters were perky, and the lady who played ragtime on the upright piano fascinated me because she never had sheet music in front of her. Her eyes were glued to the camera as her fingers flew over the keys. Bobby, the dancer with "happy feet," always smiled while effortlessly lifting and twirling his partner across the floor.

My plan worked for about a year. I got pictures in the mail from James Arness (AKA Matt Dillon, gun-toting sheriff of Dodge City on the TV western "Gun Smoke"). A few others who responded to my signed picture requests were, Ricky Nelson (dreamy youngest son on the "Ozzie and Harriet" show), Sandra Dee (nicknamed, Gidget, in beach movies), and Dinah Shore who wanted to "see the USA in her Chevrolet." All their signatures were stamped on the pictures, except for… you guessed it, Lawrence Welk's. I could tell he actually signed his name by running my fingers across it. His signature was bumpy, not smooth like the others.

Eventually my letter writing hobby wore off. Like a typical kid, I found another interest to pursue. If I remember correctly, it still involved sending and receiving mail. I wrote to all the state capitals requesting free brochures. It's a wonder I didn't become a travel agent, considering all the maps and pamphlets I got from the various states.

As time went by, going to the mailbox lost its appeal. Guess you could say the "mail lost its mystique." Now, as a senior citizen, I almost dread getting it. Maybe that's because all I seem to receive these days are bills and advertisements. Although, I must admit, Christmas cards and letters are still, most certainly appreciated.

Follow-the-Leader

The Thanksgiving/Christmas travel season is the time when thousands of Americans take to the highways in order to spend time with loved ones. One specific holiday season our youngest daughter, Ali, her husband, Rob, and their two little sweetie pies drove almost nine hours in bumper-to-bumper traffic to be with family in Washington D.C.

I wouldn't say I was a nervous wreck, but I really didn't relax until they were home, safe and sound in Henry County, Ohio. I'm not sure why I'm such a "worry wart" when family members are on the road. Maybe it's because today's traffic goes excessively fast.

Maybe it's because today's roads are excessively crowded. Maybe it's because many of today's drivers are excessively distracted; concentrating more on their Facebook friends than the road. That's why I say, "Thank heavens for satellite maps!"

Remember the days when all you could do was follow the route on a paper map or atlas? Usually the print was so small you needed a magnifying glass to read the words. Do you also remember when you had to follow hand-written directions while simultaneously driving? Thankfully those days are gone. Nowadays, a screen displays an easy-to-read map, and a clear voice tells drivers when to reroute, when to change lanes, or when to take an exit ramp.

In years past, there were occasions when only one person in a car caravan possessed specific directions to a particular place. Consequently, all other drivers joined the "conga, car line" to "follow-the-leader."

Follow-the-Leader

Getting to a destination depended upon two principles. The lead driver had to stay focused on the followers, and followers had to stay focused on the lead driver... AT ALL TIMES, NO MATTER WHAT!

Many years ago, close to a holiday weekend, Anita, my middle daughter, had a basketball tournament in Lansing, Michigan. Parents and players met in Findlay, Ohio. The coach, our fearless, self-appointed lead driver, was the only person with directions. He reassuringly said, "Don't worry. I'll keep an eye on your car from my rearview mirror. I won't let you out of my sight. Just follow close. You'll be fine."

Famous last words! Why I didn't ask for directions, I'll never know. For the first hour and a half we were "fine," just like he predicted. He drove at a steady pace, avoided lane changes, and he didn't zoom through yellow lights. Then, for no apparent reason, he turned into Mario Andretti, the champion race car driver. It was as if he forgot about little old me, chugging along behind.

Perhaps he desperately needed to use the restroom, but for some unknown reason he pressed on his accelerator and zipped around several cars. As if possessed, he began weaving in and out, crisscrossing lanes. I completely lost sight of his car. To make matters worse, darkness set in. If you've ever struggled to follow one particular set of taillights among hundreds, you know it's an impossible task. At night, all lights look alike!

I asked everyone in the car to "be quiet" so I could concentrate. I clenched my teeth, while white knuckles tightly squeezed the steering wheel. My brain ached and my heart pounded. I said a silent prayer and strained my eyes to catch a glimpse of our coach's car. Helpless, I continued to be swept along the highway with other nameless drivers, in the darkness, in bumper-to-bumper holiday traffic.

Follow-the-Leader

Worst of all, I had no clue where I was going. I only knew I was on a crowded interstate highway, speeding north in Michigan. The way things were going, Canada would be next, then Santa's workshop at the North Pole. I couldn't call our fearless leader on my cell phone because, at this time, they only existed in "Star Trek" movies. Suddenly, out of the blue, someone in the back seat leaned forward, pointed and called out, "There! Take that exit, NOW! I've seen it before. It's near the sports complex where we'll play tomorrow."

I almost cried tears of joy, but resisted, knowing blurry vision wouldn't help my situation. We all arrived safely, but I vowed to never again drive without directions. After dragging my limp body into our motel, I phoned home and confessed to my husband how frightened I had been that night.

From then on, this Nervous Nelly routinely and humbly prays for her family's safe return from daily travels, and gives thanks to God when prayers are answered. I admit I don't like everything about modern technology, but I say "Hallelujah" to computer-generated map apps. Thankfully, it's because of them, drivers no longer need to blindly play "Follow-the-Leader."

Time Travelers

FUNNY HOW CERTAIN things - simple things - remind you of your past; suddenly transporting you back in time. It might be a touch, like the silky-smooth banister inside a historic building. It might be a sound, like the rhythmic ticking of a kitchen clock's pendulum. It might be a scent, like quilts stored in a cedar chest. It might be a song; a Christmas carol heard over your car radio. It might be a taste, like the sugary goodness of grandma's freshly baked coffee cake. You never know what will trigger a specific image or feeling from years gone by. When the sensation of going back in time strikes, you have little warning, but, when it happens, it's as if you're instantly wrapped in a cozy blanket of fond memories and contentment.

It seems the more candles I add to my birthday cake, the more I reminisce about my past. From talking to other senior citizens, I don't think I'm unique. Most members of the gray-haired gang seem to enjoy thinking about life in their more youthful days. Perhaps that's because we have more years behind than ahead of us. At any rate, remembering the past gives me comfort, which is probably why I like rummaging through antique shops.

A while back I was checking out the musty, dusty shelves of an antique shop in Defiance, Ohio. I started making a mental list of items once found in everyday life, items no longer used or needed. Seeing small, glass milk bottles made me think of sitting in my school's lunchroom, struggling to pick off the bottle's shiny, thick, tinfoil cap. My second grade teacher made us save the caps throughout the year. With the addition of string and paint, we magically transformed them into Christmas ornaments.

We were pretty good at recycling back then. After our morning milk break, all students dutifully placed empty bottles into a partitioned wooden crate. The crates were loaded up and hauled away. The sterilized, refilled bottles returned to school where students once again purchased one glass bottle of white or chocolate milk for two copper pennies.

When I discovered a hall-tree loaded with women's hats, it made me think of church. Years ago, it would have been unthinkable for a lady to enter church without a hat or scarf covering her head. I took a brown pill box hat off the hook, put it on, and looked in the mirror. With its stiff netting shielding my eyes, I could have sworn I saw my mom's reflection smiling back at me.

Resting on a shelf close to the hats was a collection of white gloves. Gloves were once an important part of every female's wardrobe. Not only grown women, but little girls wore gloves on special occasions. I slipped on a pair. As if by magic my hands looked elegant, slender, and more youthful. That's probably because the gloves helped hide my age- spots and wrinkles.

Then there were handkerchiefs; lots and lots of either men's large and plain, or women's dainty, embroidered handkerchiefs. Years ago, every five-and-dime store carried a wide variety from which to choose. Back then, people didn't have Kleenex tissues, so a cloth handkerchief was an important part of daily hygiene. Men stuffed them in their pockets, and women folded them to keep inside their purse. Like inexpensive perfume and after-shave, handkerchiefs were the affordable "go to" Christmas gifts for kids to buy their parents.

Time Travelers

Vintage Samsonite suitcases are also a thing of the past. I spotted two blue specimens resting beside a worn-out wicker rocker. Compared to the rocker, they looked like new. An identical set had been my high school graduation gift over five decades earlier. They accompanied my husband and me on our honeymoon, and two years later they flew with us on a Christmas trip to visit my Aunt Leona in Texas.

These suitcases were rugged, sturdy, and next to impossible to destroy. However, they were also stiff, heavy, and awkward to carry. I remember stuffing them so full of clothes I had to sit on the lid while Bruce struggled to lock the silver, metal latches. Where are my suitcases now? They're not sitting empty in some antique shop. No sir! I've put mine to good use. They're stacked in our attic, packed full of unidentified black-and-white photographs. Someday my kids can decide what to do with both the suitcases and the pictures.

For today's younger generation, the "here and now" will eventually transform into the "good old days." It makes me wonder. As we travel through time, will antique shops exist, or will they be replaced entirely by online shopping and drone home delivery? If they do remain, what will they contain? More importantly, what items inside will trigger fond, heartwarming memories for this next generation, the Country Cousin generation? Only time will tell.

Christmas Truce

THE FOLLOWING TRUE story is not one of our family's Christmas stories, but it's an inspirational story worth retelling. It's been years since I sat in Hamler High School's World History class, so my knowledge of circumstances surrounding WWI are sketchy at best. For this Christmas story to make sense in my head I needed additional background information. I began a fact search. The following information is a brief overview of what I found.

World War I, also known as "The Great War," began in July of 1914 over a confrontation between Austria/Hungary and Serbia. It spread rapidly throughout Europe, as countries taking sides were drawn into conflict. By November of that same year, the German advance threatening France had been stopped. However, French, Belgian, and British Allied forces were unable to push the Germans completely out of France. A stalemate resulted, and both sides started digging trenches.

Warring forces hastily dug a network of defensive trenches stretching for miles from "the edge of the English Channel to the border of Switzerland." Ground between trenches, called "No-Man's-Land," often separated opposing armies by less than one hundred feet. "The enemy troops were so close they could hear each other talk and smell their cooking." Soldiers on both sides were trapped with nowhere to go. Frostbite was common. It was here during the bleak, wet winter of 1914 men prayed they wouldn't get hit by sniper fire. It was here, in the midst of war, the stage was set for peace.

What exactly happened on Christmas Eve and Christmas Day of 1914? Oral accounts, diary entries, and letters tell of soldiers from both sides leaving their rifles behind and crawling out of the trenches to celebrate Christmas with their enemy. Nobody knows exactly how it all began or how it spread, but eventually two-thirds of all troops, an estimated one hundred thousand soldiers, are believed to have participated in this legendary unauthorized ceasefire.

Troops exchanged Christmas carols and stories. In a "New York Times" interview, British soldier Graham Williams observed, "First the Germans would sing one of their carols and then we would sing one of ours. I thought, well this is really a most extraordinary thing, two nations both singing in the middle of a war." According to British corporal John Ferguson, "We shook hands, wished each other a Merry Christmas, and were soon conversing as if we had known each other for years. Here we were laughing and chatting to men whom only a few hours before we were trying to kill."

There were impromptu soccer matches, using cans or small sandbags as make-shift balls. In one recorded instance a British soldier even had his hair cut by his pre-war German barber. Mortal enemies exchanged small gifts such as cigarettes, chocolates, sausages, buttons, hats, and food. British soldier Frank Richards remembered, "German soldiers even rolled barrels of beer seized from a nearby brewery across No-Man's-Land to the British trenches where we raised toasts to one another's health." The Christmas Truce also gave both sides the opportunity to retrieve and bury dead comrades whose frozen bodies had lain for weeks on barren, desolate land between trenches.

As the sun set and Christmas Day ended, peace also ended, and the fighting resumed. When Christmas came to the trenches in

1915, those in charge made sure the unofficial truce did not return. Commanding officers from both sides issued orders that such a "grassroots ceasefire" would never be allowed to happen again.

The United States entered the war in August of 1917. Two years later the war ended. World War I took the lives of more than nine million soldiers with twenty-one million more wounded. I think you would agree, all those who bravely played a role in the Christmas Truce of 1914 participated in a life-changing, awe-inspiring event. Here's praying future Christmases bring everlasting "Peace on Earth."

Family Gathering Part I

CHRISTMAS IS A time for families to gather, but what if family members are scattered far and wide? Then the gathering becomes a matter of logistics, and practical questions arise. There are questions such as, how will so many people manage to come together at the same time? Where will everyone sleep? What activities will be planned to pass the time? Most importantly, which family member will step up to the plate, take the reindeer by the antlers, and coordinate all the details?

Many years ago, my sister and brother-in-law boldly faced this ultimate Christmas challenge and managed to gather us all under one roof for three full days in December. Looking back, we should have taken up a collection to buy them a well-deserved vacation to the Bahamas once their whole ordeal was over. If it's any consolation, they provided everyone with unforgettable memories of a fairy tale Christmas that can never be duplicated. Join me in a "blast from the past" as I step back in time to the Christmas of 1978.

Several years earlier, my sister and her family moved to a one hundred thirty-year-old, five-bedroom, rambling farmhouse located between Trumansburg and Ithaca, New York. The house, which at one time had been part of a much larger estate, rested on a hill surrounded by forty acres of land containing a woods, pond, orchard, hiking trails, small fields, and a stone foundation double-barn. If you sat on the front porch or parted the lace curtains of the bedroom windows, you could see a wide patch of blue in the distance: Lake Cayuga-one of the five Finger Lakes.

This rural setting was an abrupt change for the occupants of the house. All previous homes had been in urban, university towns, but when my brother-in-law accepted a position to teach at Cornell, they packed up their three boys and traded in their street shoes for farm boots. From the moment they moved in, I think my sister saw it as the perfect place to have a family gathering.

Organization for this get-together began that summer. After lots of phone calls, the date was set. (I'm pretty sure it was etched in stone.) This allowed family members flying from Texas and Florida the chance to book early flights. Planning the trip required a major effort by everyone, but the Ohio branch of the family had it comparatively easy. All we had to do was patiently wait for the day to arrive so we could pack up, gas up, and drive ten hours through three states in Christmas traffic. No holiday airport anxiety for us.

The Christmas countdown began. Everyone kept fingers and toes crossed, hoping that, after all the pre-date orchestration, everything would fall into place. With so many people involved, it was easy to imagine something going wrong. We were taking no chances. As a precaution (afraid our aging compact station wagon might conk out along the way) my husband borrowed his parents' car for our long trek to the northeast.

Fortunately for us, my sister was all set in New York with big-ticket items such as a baby crib and highchair, but packing for a one-year-old in the depths of winter was still a challenge. Diapers, formula, bottles, Gerber's jars, and lots of warm baby clothes were added to our grown-up stash of necessities. The car was loaded. We were ready, and New York was ready for all of us.

Family Gathering Part I

Anticipation and excitement made it difficult to sleep, so I was thankful when the alarm clock finally went off. It was before dawn of the big day. Eleven months earlier, the Blizzard of 1978 made traveling impossible. With the memory of snow drifts as high as our chicken coop roof still fresh in my husband's mind, he popped open the trunk at the last minute and threw in a snow shovel, flashlight, and lots of blankets. (It's better to be safe than... well, you know.)

We made one last dash around the house to be sure nothing was forgotten. Then we turned off all but one light, locked the doors, buckled our son in his car seat, put our coffee thermos on the floor between us, pulled out of our driveway, and headed in the early morning darkness toward the gathering. At about this same time we figured others in our family would be soaring above the clouds, pointed in the same direction.

The trip was long which made arriving at our destination all-the-more rewarding. We were the last ones to check in, and waiting for us at the door were my three New York nephews and my two young nieces from Florida, all anxious to grab their baby cousin and usher him around. The house was filled with hugs of greeting and chatter as we unloaded the car and warmed our hands by the large, crackling, brick fireplace.

My sister had a generous pot of dumpling soup simmering on the stove. The aroma of the soup mixed with the scent of several live decorated pine trees made everything seem so cozy and perfect, but real-life drama soon intervened. Nobody could have predicted what surprises the next few days would bring.

Family Gathering Part II

DAY-TO-DAY LIFE TAKES its toll on extended families, making it tough to find the perfect time and place to gather. There are obstacles, common to us all; obstacles that get in the way of gathering. Distance is often a factor. Also, jobs keep us anchored to one spot. Once that next generation reaches high school, extracurricular commitments put a screeching halt to lengthy visits. As we get older, health concerns add trauma to travel. The tempting promise of a relaxing, hassle-free holiday is enough reason for some people to hunker down and stay put.

Each member of our family was determined to accomplish the impossible; to overcome all of these obstacles and celebrate Christmas together. The year was 1978. Our seventeen-member family gathered for three days to spend Christmas in New York. Some of us, those from Florida and Texas, flew into Syracuse and arrived at my sister's farmhouse outside of Trumansburg by way of rental car. The Ohio contingent packed up and drove ten hours to the Land of the Finger Lakes.

Even though the century-old dwelling had five bedrooms, many of the other rooms became makeshift sleeping quarters. That first night you could hear lighthearted voices echo, "Good night, Jim Bob. Good night, John Boy" in homage to the then-popular TV series "The Waltons." The following morning everyone lingered over breakfast, exchanging family stories while lounging around in cozy pajamas, sipping hot mulled cider.

It was about this time when I noticed our one-year-old son's chubby cheeks looking especially rosy-red and his forehead feeling warm to the touch. The thermometer indicated a 101 degree fever. We hustled him to my sister's pediatrician who diagnosed, "an ear infection." I guess you could say the timing was perfect. If he had shown symptoms one day sooner, we never would have started out. Thank heavens for antibiotics. Crisis averted.

That evening was girls' night out. In support of a local theater, my sister bought us all fundraiser tickets to see a live performance of "The Nutcracker." Dutifully I stayed behind with the guys and our sick baby. As it turned out, all I missed were numb fingers and toes. The purpose of this performance was to raise money for the theater's broken-down furnace. Who knew a faulty furnace meant no heat? Instead of applause, the performers heard chattering teeth.

On day two of this once-in-a-lifetime gathering, my Aunt Leona from Texas and my brother's mother-in-law from Florida each came down with a severe case of stomach flu. Needless to say, both spent the entire day in bed, inches away from a bucket. Later that same evening, it began to snow. It snowed, and it snowed... big, beautiful flakes.

By the next morning, Christmas Eve Day, fourteen inches of the white fluffy stuff blanketed everything. The setting looked like a Thomas Kinkade winter wonderland painting. My Florida nieces, never having experienced snow, were thrilled. My sister, alias Martha Stewart, had purchased snowsuits, boots, and gloves... just in case. So, they bundled up and made their first snow angels. Their larger-than-life snowman truly had magical powers. Not wanting to miss the fun, the two ladies who had been feeling under the weather, perked up and peeked out the windows in order to snap pictures of dapper old Frosty.

When Christmas morning rolled around, everyone was feeling fit as a fiddle. Things were looking up. We exchanged presents by the fireplace amid soft music and laughter. Then we all sat around the large harvest table, making short work of the delicious egg casserole breakfast. Knowing we'd soon be heading home made us all feel a bit introspective and nostalgic. Nobody wanted this morning to end.

We each planned to prepare for our last full day by taking turns using the bathroom's shower. That's when disaster struck. There was no water! My brother-in-law went to the basement and switched fuses. No luck! Suspecting the well had dried up from overuse, he tried Plan B. He switched to cistern water, only to discover it too was bone dry. Implementing Plan C, he located a driver willing to deliver cistern water on Christmas Day. Things were looking up! A solution seemed to be near! But, when making the turn into the farmhouse driveway, the truck slid sideways, landing in a deep, snowy ditch across the road. Thankfully the driver wasn't hurt.

Seeing our predicament, a kindly neighbor rushed over with his tractor and chains to rescue the fully loaded tank truck. I've often wondered if the drivers were aware of the entertainment they provided. Could they see the many curious faces staring, with noses pressed against the windows? Once the cistern was filled, we looked on in anticipation as my sister, standing in the kitchen, turned the sink's faucet. Nope! Nothing! Nada! Zilch! No water! Plan D resulted in a plumber replacing a faulty pump with a new one. Aha, a Christmas miracle, lifesaving liquid! We offered the plumber/magician an honorary family membership. He declined.

Early the next morning, with not-so-hidden sighs of relief, my sister and brother-in-law waved good-bye to their guests. Looking back, I realize the special significance of this gathering. It can never ever be

Family Gathering Part II

repeated because, sadly, several family members are no longer with us. This makes me cherish even more the memories and pictures of those few crazy, special, wonderful days spent together as one big, relatively happy family. After all, being part of any large family gathering means appreciating good times while putting up with times that are not so good. Here's wishing you all a memory-filled gathering.

Pocketknife Possibilities

THIS HOLIDAY SEASON I'm aiming to be thankful for the little things in life. You know, those everyday things, those mundane things we take for granted, things like pocketknives. Seriously! This small tool has often come to my rescue, but I've never taken the time to think much about it, let alone be grateful for it... that is, until now.

If you live on a farm, you already recognize the value and versatility of this device. When my husband comes in from work, he empties his pockets and places the contents on a small table. It's always the same stuff. First, out comes his wallet, next his pocketknife, and finally he removes his loose change.

He places it all side-by-side where it's easily retrieved in the morning.

Each evening I do my husband a big favor by scooping up the change. Honestly, he doesn't miss the money. It helps keep his pockets organized and, frankly, I like to collect coins. However, I wouldn't dream of touching his wallet or pocketknife. There's no question his wallet is important because it holds his driver's license and credit cards, but what's so great about his pocketknife?

If I had a nickel for all the times I've watched my husband walk in a field, bend down and dig through the soil with his pocketknife, I'd need a much bigger container for my confiscated coins. What's he looking for? With the sharp point of the steel tip he digs for germinating seeds or variations of moisture in the soil. When his search is over, he wipes the blade on his jeans, folds it back into its compact case, then stuffs it into the deepest part of his pocket so it won't fall out.

Pocketknife Possibilities

Now you know why a pocketknife is important to my husband, but what does any of this have to do with me? Why should I be thankful for a pocketknife? Again, if I had a nickel for each time I've said, "Honey, could you come here with your pocketknife?" I wouldn't be rich, but I'd be richer. He and his blade buddy have "saved my day" on multiple occasions.

When I need to cut through thick plastic, string, or thin wire, I call on my husband and his trusty pocketknife. When it's autumn and we're outside under the apple tree, his pocketknife slices the fruit so every grandchild gets an equal piece. When I'm having a tough time opening thick envelopes, his pocketknife works wonders. When there's no screwdriver around, his pocketknife makes a good substitute. When I want to gather lilacs or wildflowers for an indoor arrangement, his pocketknife cuts through tough stems.

A couple of years ago my husband and I went shopping in an antique store in Auburn, Indiana. I focused on the Depression Ware while my husband was transfixed on a glass case full of pocketknives. His excitement mounted and he called me over to admire the collection. Each pocketknife was unique. There were all sizes with different shaped blades and a wide variety of outside cases. Some cases were plain, while others had intricate patterns made from inlaid wood and mother-of-pearl. He bought two of the plain ones.

I asked why he needed two new pocketknives. His answer was simple. "These aren't for me, they're for our oldest grandsons, Mack and Gus. Every boy needs to know how to safely handle a pocketknife. It's a rite of passage. I'll have their names engraved on the side. It'll be a special Christmas present from their Pawpaw."

Pocketknife Possibilities

Time has passed since my husband and I went pocketknife shopping, and, once again, Christmas is around the corner. I've been thinking. Maybe we should go back to that antique store. Perhaps our three oldest granddaughters need pocketknives, too. After all, boys bake brownies. Shouldn't girls learn to use pocketknives?

Yep, this year I'm determined to be thankful for the little things life has to offer; and the unlikely "grateful to have" top contender is the pocketknife. Come to think of it, I could probably use my husband's pocketknife to carve our Christmas turkey. In my mind, the short sturdy blade would be easier to control than that long, unwieldy carving knife we normally use. It would be faster to sharpen, and it'd take up less space in my jam-packed kitchen drawer.

Who knows, maybe this year I'll get lucky and find a pocketknife in my Christmas stocking. I would be truly thankful, but honestly, my oldest three granddaughters, Evie, Meyta, and Cece... probably not so much!

Guilty as Charged

THERE ARE SOME things in life that encourage me to reflect on the past. For instance, familiar songs, old family photos, and outdated clothes hanging in my closet all lure my thoughts back to a time and place that exists only in my memory. A few Christmases ago, I was zapped back to another time, and it was not due to any of the three things just listed. It was all because of a movie: the rerun of the holiday classic, "Home Alone." In between the giggles and chuckles, the film made me squirm in my seat. The story line, as the old saying goes, "hit too close to home," pushing forward forgotten guilt.

"Possible, but not probable" was the common consensus when the film first flashed on the big silver screen decades ago. Even if the mix-up was unintentional, no mother in her right mind could leave a child behind while the entire family gleefully trooped out of the house, climbed into a taxi, boarded a plane, and left the country for a Christmas vacation... right?

Wrong! I, for one, know it is entirely possible for a loving mother to unwittingly leave her child stranded and helplessly left to his or her own devices. So, my advice of the day is, don't be too quick to judge the mother in the movie, even though her guilt, unlike mine, did seem to evaporate the second she walked into her house/mansion. (FYI, the house of my dreams.)

By now you have correctly guessed that I, at some point in my younger years, suffered the trauma of leaving my duckling in its nest, my colt in its stall, my cub in its den... well, you get the picture. More accurately, I left my small fry (the name of a baby fish) behind in its school. Yep, I was teaching third grade. My son was a kindergartener, on an every-other-day schedule. For this particular day, he was instructed to meet me in my classroom after school.

But when he got there, I was nowhere to be found. I had left the building and was zipping around, running errands in a nearby town. Twenty minutes later, realizing what I had done, I broke out in a cold sweat. My heart started to pound, and my ears began ringing. I couldn't turn the car around; the trip back would take too long. This was before cell phones, so I stopped at the nearest store, asked to use their phone, called the school, and was relieved to hear my son was happily playing checkers with my friend, a fellow fifth grade teacher.

Until I saw the rerun of "Home Alone" for the second time, my plan to ditch the guilt and forget the whole thing worked. If the incident was ever brought up at family gatherings, I would quickly plead the fifth and change the topic of conversation. After all, "What's done is done!" My son turned out normal, so there were no lasting ill effects as far as I could see.

Me? I honestly do suffer from occasional guilt, but over the years I've come to accept guilt as part of being a mother. In the words of the late Erma Bombeck, "Guilt, the gift that keeps on giving." Well, now, I'm wondering… is guilt part of being a grandmother too?

Kitchen Cowgirl

Howdy, Pardners! When I was knee-high to a "jackrabbit" I dreamed of bein' a cowgirl like Dale Evans. Seems in some odd way my wish came true. Ladies, when rustlin' up Thanksgiving and Christmas vittles for your posse, have you ever noticed folks gather in or near your kitchen? My kitchen's small, about the size of a large chuck wagon. There's barely room for one cowgirl to work at a time; yet, sure as shootin', that's where my gang wants to linger to "chew the fat" or "shoot the breeze."

I recollect my first big mistake. In the past, I always put the appetizers close to where I was workin'. By golly, that was the wrong thing to do! When I finally realized my grazin' guests didn't mosey on, it was too late. I tried to imitate Clint Eastwood in the old "Rawhide" TV western, but any attempt to "head 'em up and move 'em out" backfired.

For instance, after some ponderin' on the situation, I put the appetizers in "greener pastures" throughout the homestead. My intention was to get folks to spread out, meander, and follow the grub. Dag gum it, this plan failed because apparently there are two kinds of cowpokes. Here's what happened...

First, there were the "homebodies," those who refused to budge. Guess they didn't want to spoil their appetites with pre-meal munchin', so they planted their boots firmly right where I was workin'. The second group, the "food-finders," fanned out to chow down on chips and salsa, then boomeranged back to rejoin the others. Once again, my kitchen and prep area was packed with people. I've learned it's next to impossible to herd contented, chattin', chewin' cowpokes on any kind of trail drive.

Don't get me wrong. I love preparin' food for kin folk and friends, just don't fence me in. Give me some elbow room, please. It's difficult to properly rustle up grub when bumpin' into someone's "beehind" at every turn. It makes me feel like Calamity Jane. To open-up the refrigerator or oven door means someone has to dance the "Boot Skootin' Boogie" just to "kindly, get out of my way." The sink, microwave, and dishwasher are crammed together. You can bet a fifty-dollar gold piece some chit-chatin' buckaroo is blockin' my path to an easy access.

I don't mean to "ruffle any feathers," but there's another situation I need to gab about. Bein' surrounded by an audience when fixin' a feast makes me self-conscious. To have hungry eyes watchin' as I carve a turkey makes me nervous. It's as if I'm in the center ring of a rodeo, tryin' to stay seated on a buckin' bronco. That's why I'm careful to pitch the mashed potato boxes before all the wranglers arrive. I don't want guests to know my taters aren't prepared from scratch; that they're made compliments of Bob Evans and not Cowgirl Konnie. The way I figure it, "What they don't know won't hurt 'em."

There are always those well-meanin' city slickers who offer to help out, but I kindly refuse. After all, it would be rude for the hostess of the shindig to say, "If you really want to help, you have eight seconds to grab your lariat, lasso the whole darn bunch, and drag 'em away from my kitchen!" Instead, I answer with, "Thanks, there's only enough elbow room for one. Besides, I have a hankerin' to do it myself."

My kids advise me not to be so cantankerous. They say I need to "chill out!" They suggested I meditate or listen to soft music before the kitchen chaos begins. I told 'em us cowgirls live by one motto, "Speak your mind, then ride away on a fast horse." My kids pointed out I don't even have a slow horse. By jiggers, they're right!

So, in the future, I'll take their advice. As a woman with true grit, I'll remain unruffled. I'll calmly cook the grub in my cramped, confined quarters with all eyes watchin'. When everyone's ready to ride off into the sunset, I'll breathe a sigh of relief, smile, wave, and say in my sweetest cowgirl voice, "Y'all come back now! Hear?"

Wedding Wisdom

June is typically known as the month of weddings. In 1948 there was even a movie starring Bette Davis and Robert Montgomery called "June Bride." Warm, sunny June may be known as the best month for couples to "tie the knot," but it's during the cold month of December couples are likely to begin the marriage process. On Christmas, cupid has been known to pick up his bow and let arrows fly. Take an informal survey of your friends and relatives. I'll bet many of them said "Yes!" to a marriage proposal on Christmas. I know I did.

Once a love-struck couple agrees to get "hitched," the enormity of their commitment sets in. By commitment, I don't mean the prospect of spending the rest of their lives together as husband and wife. The commitment I'm referring to is the prospect of planning and paying for the "often expensive" upcoming event. Nowadays, coordinating the wedding and all it encompasses has become a major production that rivals many low-budget movies.

In days gone by, when life was slower and things were simpler, weddings were cheaper. Commonly, the vows were exchanged in a local church. Receptions were small, intimate gatherings. If you were lucky enough to have any honeymoon at all, your romantic getaway consisted of a weekend trip to a nearby big city.

One main reason engaged couples faced fewer expenses is because years ago there were fewer choices. Today the betrothed must decide whether-or-not they want their ceremony to be recorded, their reception to be organized by a wedding planner, and their honeymoon to be at an "all inclusive" resort. These budget-busting choices just didn't exist decades ago.

(Here's a "mother-of-the-bride" budget saving hint. Consider having the actual wedding during the Christmas season. Our middle daughter, Ali, reduced wedding decorating dollars by saying, "I do," a few days after Christmas. The church was splendidly decked out in the spirit of the holidays, and using seasonal decor made planning a reception less complicated.)

A few years back I had the pleasure of chatting with friends, an older, local couple about area weddings. They said, "Years ago in rural Henry County, Ohio, receptions were commonly held in barns, and on some occasions guests supplied food by bringing potluck dishes." They attended one such barn reception in the middle of winter. A polka band provided music. Only trouble was, on this night, the temperature dropped, and all the instruments froze. Undeterred by this minor setback, the newlyweds simply moved the party into the house.

At another wedding, a reception was held on the second floor of the Hamler Hardware. The groom hired someone to take care of his cows during the festivities. This person did what he was told, but after completing the chores, he forgot to close the cows' gate. Big mistake!

That evening, around 9:30, a train, the Capital Limited going from Chicago to North Baltimore, roared by, hitting several cows which had wandered onto the tracks. News soon reached the revelers. The reception abruptly ended, but resumed bright and early the next morning with friends and neighbors all pitching in to butcher the beef.

Years ago, if a young married couple skipped having a reception, they could count on having the surprise of a lifetime: a belling.

Wedding Wisdom

At a belling, the newlyweds were unexpectedly summoned by a group of well-wishers honking horns, banging pots and pans, and calling for the stunned couple to "come and join the party!" This racket was often accompanied by a shotgun blast fired into the air. The couple was then expected to welcome the partyers into their house or barn.

If this wasn't an option, the guests packed up the merriment, music, and munchies and took it all to a nearby establishment where the celebration continued into the wee hours of the morning. At one such belling, the shotgun blast accidentally hit the power line, cutting off all electricity to the couple's house and barn. Everyone stood there in shocked silence. (No pun intended.) Undeterred, the party then moved to a nearby location with light.

Christmastime is a time for marriage proposals. Wedding plans will soon follow. The cold, hard, fact is, having a fancy "schmancy" wedding doesn't guarantee the marriage will last. Some of the most common, inexpensive weddings produced marriages that have withstood the test of time. On the other hand, some of the most lavish, costly weddings have ended before all wedding bills were paid.

There's one piece of wisdom the couple I interviewed wanted to share with those who are newly engaged. They both agreed, "You don't have to spend a ton of money on a wedding to have a ton of fun!" After being married for over sixty years, I guess this couple would know. So folks, I feel safe in saying, "You can take their advice to the bank!"

My Version of an Excursion

ONCE CHRISTMAS IS in the record books, it soon becomes time to pack away artificial trees, decorations, and lights. In the blink on an eye, life gets back to normal. So, before we settle into the new year, how about taking one last gander at the beauty of the Christmas season?

A few days after Christmas, my husband and I were sitting in the living room. As is often the case, we had eaten an early supper, but I wasn't quite ready to slip into my jammies and call it a night. It seemed way too early to be nodding off to dreamland, snoring away in our recliners.

Doubtful I'd get a favorable response, but ever hopeful, I looked over at my hubby and said, "How about driving around to look at Christmas lights?" His reply surprised me. "Sounds like a good idea!" (I'm counting this as a Christmas miracle.) There was one small catch. He would go only if I agreed to drive.

I didn't tell him, but I had planned on driving all along. From experience, I've learned whoever sits behind the wheel is the mile master; the car captain. If my husband had driven, our trip would have been super short. We would have been back home before you could say, "Kris Kringle." Since I was in the driver's seat, he surrendered all control, making me this excursion's executive decision-maker.

We shuffled to our garage and car wearing slippers and sweatshirts, ready for the evening's adventure. I pulled out of our driveway,

My Version of an Excursion

heading toward Deshler, the nearest small town. While driving along the darkened country roads, we enjoyed the wide variety of illuminated farmhouses and trees. We observed that some people decorate their property by sticking to a theme or a simple color pattern. On the other hand, some people focused on volume. Either way, the outcome was splendid.

Nearing the north end of town, we saw glowing spheres in the distance. As we got closer, the beauty of the floating lights seemed magical. I've since been informed the owner makes these spheres by hand. What started out as a few lighted orbs, suspended from one tree, has since blossomed to encompass two houses, two entire yards, and numerous trees. As the car's captain, I chose to slowly drive by the surreal scene several times.

There were many lovely displays, but there was one in particular I wanted to see. Several years earlier I had ridden with my middle daughter, Anita, and one-year-old grandson, Mack, to see lights synchronized to music, streaming from our car's radio. My husband and I were pleasantly surprised to find this unique display still going strong. We sat in our warm comfy car, eyes glued to the dancing lights, ears soaking up the sounds of the season. It was mesmerizing; it was entertaining; it was way better than sitting in front of the TV; and better yet, it was free!

Not quite ready to end this excursion, I drove by the spheres one last time, heading in the opposite direction toward home. As I zipped right on past our house, my husband said, "Hey, where are you going? Why didn't you pull into our driveway?" I replied with, "Take it easy. Relax and enjoy the ride! We'll be home in our recliners soon enough."

Our next small-town stop was Holgate. Their park had a wonderful display, with dozens of colorful Christmas blow-ups. I had seen this menagerie of cartoon characters during the day, but wondered how it looked at night, and I was not disappointed. We had fun picking out familiar faces such as The Grinch, The Minions, The Pillsbury Dough Boy, Rudolph, and the star of the display, Santa. We circled the park twice, taking it all in.

Every town, large and small, has special Christmas displays. You might find them in store windows, on streetlights, or in parks. Many people put a lot of thought and effort into decorating the outdoors. It's their seasonal gift for everyone to appreciate.

Before the calendar flips to the new year, and all the colorful lights go dark, I suggest you take a drive to celebrate these dazzling displays. It's fun! Oh, there's an additional perk. For this excursion, you can even wear your slippers and jammies, and the best part is... no one will ever know!

Penny Power

MANY PEOPLE THINK of a penny as something to be tossed aside, even discarded. I'm not one of those people. When I see a stray penny, I pick it up. Growing up, I watched my older sister, Karen, go to school sporting brand new "penny loafers" with a shiny one cent piece wedged tightly into that "peek-a-boo" slot on the top of each shoe. I could barely see Abe's profile, but in my eyes, that slight glimmer of copper added a lot of "class" to an otherwise drab shoe.

As her "little sister" I also thought those pennies on top of her shoes served no practical purpose. The way I saw it, my job was to free Abe from his "penny prison" so he and I could do what we were meant to do; which was to buy me a piece of Bazooka Bubble Gum. I usually had to wait several weeks for the new, stiff leather to soften before my little fingers could pry the coin from the slot. (Upon reading this, my sister now knows why she had to replace the pennies in her shoes so often.)

I can also attribute my fascination with pennies to my big brother, Bob, and my sister-in-law, Jan. When I was around nine, they planned for me to spend a few days with them after Christmas. The deal was, they would show me around Chicago, then allow me to shop for clothes at the giant Marshall Field's store downtown. This presented a problem. In order to shop, I needed money. I had none.

Their invitation, given in June, meant I had time to get some cold, hard cash. This required more than just a couple of pennies from my sister's loafers. What I needed now were hundreds of pennies, and I knew exactly where to get them. It was customary for Dad to come home from work and empty his "pocket change" into a bowl on our dining room table.

When I heard about my future trip, I asked Dad if I could lay claim to all the pennies in the bowl. He answered in the affirmative, and my "penny pinching" campaign began. Each evening for the next six months, I picked out pennies and placed them in my patent-leather Easter purse. As the purse gained weight, I gained purchasing power.

The anticipated day finally arrived. Mom packed my suitcase, but before she closed the lid, I included my penny-filled purse. This "Country Mouse" was headed for the "Land of Lincoln" with exactly twenty-six dollars in Lincoln head pennies. Dad and Mom drove me to the train station in Deshler, asked the porter to "keep an eye on me," and about six hours later I was asking my brother when we could go shopping. I showed him my "loot." He acted properly impressed.

After two days of sight-seeing, we finally headed to "the store of my dreams." My brother nervously warned me not to drop my purse full of pennies on the escalator. I assured him I wasn't that clumsy and immediately tightened my grip. My sister-in-law helped me choose three skirts.

I walked up to a clerk and showed her my form of payment. What a champ! Without hesitation, she dumped my coins on the counter. We all began stacking. When there were ten piles of ten pennies the clerk systematically scooped them into a box. It took time, but eventually enough copper dollars were dumped into the box to pay for the skirts. I left the store with a full shopping bag and an empty purse.

Flash forward some twenty-five years. Our eleven-year-old middle daughter, Anita, wanted a Nintendo for Christmas. My husband and I discourage her from including it on her Christmas wish list for three specific reasons: she was too young, it was too expensive, and playing it entailed sitting and staring at a TV screen. She remembered hearing my "Chicago penny pinching" story and asked if she could try to save pennies to buy it herself. We answered in the affirmative, and her "Nintendo penny pinching" campaign began.

Each evening, for the next two years, she picked out pennies in the spare-change bowl in our dining room. She dropped them into a large plastic jug. As the jug gained weight, she gained purchasing power, and eventually she saved over one hundred dollars in pennies; enough to buy that Nintendo. Her three children, Mack, Meyta, and Malone, still enjoy playing with it these many years later.

So, now you know why, whenever I see a lone penny on a sidewalk, I make the effort to pick it up. From experience I've learned, every penny has potential.

Trash Talk

IT'S THAT TIME of year when the football season's winding down and the basketball season's gearing up. The NBA (National Basketball Association) is noted for its "trash talking" players. These professionals are athletes who not only play the physical game on the court, but they try to bolster their chances of winning by getting into the heads of their opponents.

Historically, Larry Bird is considered the champion of trash talk. For example, in a three-point shootout, Bird notoriously said to his opposition, "I hope all you guys are thinking about second place, because I'm winning this!" It wasn't just bravado on his part. He backed up his trash talk with actions that produced positive results, making him a powerful force to be reckoned with.

I hope the revelation I'm about to disclose isn't too disappointing to male readers, but this story isn't about my lead-in. It's not about basketball; it's not about Larry Bird; and it's not about the kind of talk used as ammunition during the game of "hoops." Nope! In this story I simply want to talk about trash. That's right - trash; otherwise known as garbage.

Christmas is over and my sights are aimed at our own personal "Mount Trashmore." I've watched this mountain of rubbish grow like a volcano in the corner of our garage. Our giant waste containers were full to the brim, so the only thing left to do was start a separate pile of bagged-up trash. There it is: one shiny, black, mountain of throw-away, paper stuff looming in the corner, waiting for refuse collectors to arrive.

My question is, "How did this happen?" Could it be, over the years, changes in packing materials have helped increase our volume of trash? Toys used to come in flimsy cardboard containers. Nowadays they're packaged in thick, heavy-duty cardboard boxes. The toys inside are then wrapped in stiff, thick, unbendable plastic, making each package as impenetrable as a Brinks armored truck.

Volume is the key word here. On Christmas Day, after all the presents were unwrapped, the volume of trash accumulated by nine grandkids and eight adults filled two extra-large trash bags. Honestly, I think the kids had as much fun scooping up paper, boxes, and wrapping off the floor as they did playing with their gifts. It became a competition to see who could gather the most trash to jam into the bags.

Years ago, before trash volume was an issue, every house in every town had an inconspicuous backyard alleyway. This narrow path ran the length of the block and was used for the sole purpose of trash collection. It was here that each household placed two small, silver, metal garbage cans with lids. Inside the cans, trash was put in paper grocery bags. (Large plastic bags weren't used until the early 1970's.) It's hard to believe these two little cans did the trick. They were all that was needed back then. If you lived in rural areas, you carried your trash to the backyard burn barrel, lit the match, and watched as the red glow gobbled the garbage.

Larry Bird is my husband's hero. Not because he was the king of trash talk on the basketball court, but because he always did what he said he would do. He backed up his trash talk with actions that got positive results. My husband is my hero. Why? Because he does what he says he will do. When I remind him to lug the big plastic bags to the corner of the garage, he does it. Not always cheerfully, but he does it!

Trash Talk

In conclusion, my life lesson for this story is, "like trash talk, talking about trash should always be backed up by positive actions that lead to positive results." Christmas is over. Thankfully, our Mount Trashmore is no longer a Henry County landmark. That is, until next Christmas!

TV Transformation

LAST YEAR, OUR son, Ryan, and daughter-in-law, Andrea, gave us an Amazon Fire Stick for Christmas. A week later our son stopped over to set it up; to help us get started; to show us how it worked. Not that many years ago, giving us a "fire stick" would have meant we received kindling or a lighter to help jumpstart a flame in our fireplace.

This newfangled application of familiar words seems to have no relationship to the original meaning. So, here we were, gathered not in front of our fireplace, but in front of our flat-screen television to learn what we must do to double our programming pleasure.

I really tried hard to focus on our son's instructions so he wouldn't have to go over the same thing multiple times, but I have to admit my mind wandered. My thoughts flashed back to 1957, to my first grade classroom at Horace Mann Elementary in Lima, Ohio.

It was here that my teacher, Mrs. Hullinger, asked the little girls (each wearing a dress, anklets, and Buster Brown shoes), as well as the little boys (wearing khaki pants, belts, and button-down shirts), to raise their hands if they had a television set in their home. I felt sorry for those unfortunate classmates who sat with hands folded on their desk.

Back then, owning a TV was a really big deal. Our prized small, upright rectangular box was the focal point of our living room. With its greenish, glass screen on top, plastic knobs in the middle, and thick, woven cloth hiding speakers on the bottom,

TV Transformation

we were introduced to the latest in electronic entertainment.

In the morning my parents started their day with NBC's early version of "Today," hosted by smooth-talking Dave Garroway. Then it was my turn to join Miss Francis ringing her hand-held bell, inviting kids to watch "Ding Dong School." This was followed by that gray-haired guy with giant pockets, Captain Kangaroo and his bib overall wearing side-kick Mr. Greenjeans.

Any student home sick, recuperating on the davenport from mumps or measles, slept through those boring afternoon soap operas but thought it was a special treat to watch the weeping winner of "Queen for a Day" get the crown and that Maytag washer and dryer of her dreams. You could rest and keep your eyes closed while listening to the often comical answers from Art Linkletter's interviews of squirmy little kids.

Back then, owning multiple TV sets was an uncommon privilege, reserved only for the rich and famous, so members of the typical American family had to agree to watch the same programs. In the evenings our family enjoyed shows such as "The Hit Parade," "The Ed Sullivan Show," "Dragnet," "Our Miss Brooks," "Have Gun Will Travel," "Rawhide," "Wagon Train," "Leave it to Beaver," and "Bonanza." Parents never had to be concerned about little eyes and ears seeing or hearing something inappropriate, because this was a time when all shows were "family friendly."

This was also a time when television stations frequently experienced "technical difficulty." The viewers were then asked, through the fixed sign on the screen, to "PLEASE STAND BY." Even the television sets themselves were less than reliable. Tubes regularly burned out, requiring a house visit from the handy-dandy TV repair man. He walked in, carrying a large, two-tiered case full of individually boxed-up glass tubes. He positioned his case next to the TV set, opened it, unscrewed the TV's back panel, and worked his magic. It was similar to a "house call" from your family doctor, minus the trauma of a shot.

A lifetime full of television has sparked some milestones along the way. Within our first five years of marriage, my husband and I traded in our cart and portable TV with tinfoil-wrapped antennae for a larger screen. The projected images were still black and white, but the polished hardwood cabinet sure looked "pretty spiffy." Eventually we made the big step up to a color console.

Then along came the remote; a device giving power and authority to anyone holding it in the palm of his/her hand. For some perverse reason I find great joy in irritating my family by asking, "Has anyone seen the button presser? It's been missing for a while." The reply goes something like, "It's NOT called a BUTTON PRESSER! It's called a REMOTE!" To which I add, "At least I don't call it a CHANNEL CHANGER like your Aunt Karen." To which someone inevitably says, "Two wrongs don't make a right! It's called a REMOTE!" After much searching, I usually find the "whatchama-callit" sandwiched between the padded arm and seat of my recliner.

The beginning of a new year is a good time to plan for the future, but it's also a good time to reflect on the past. With this newfangled fire-stick in hand, I look forward to a future full of more diverse TV viewing. Also, with this newfangled fire-stick in hand, I looked back at our son, Ryan, and asked, "Would you mind going over all the instructions once again? Guess I wasn't really paying attention that first time."

Action or Inaction?

With a new year just around the corner, the holiday hoopla is slowly winding down. For some of us, specifically members of the gray-haired gang, this means we can now relax and just sit. As we age, limited mobility can make doing everyday activities seem more difficult, so any opportunity to simply sit becomes irresistible.

Here's a scenario of what can happen. We've spent a restless, uncomfortable night. Then we drag ourselves out of bed. Immediately our joints ache. Our muscles feel stiff. Our entire body hurts, making it a chore to move. So, what do we do? We head to the medicine cabinet, take an Aleve, and then we sit. And we sit some more.

I'm here to warn readers to resist. Don't give in to this urge to sit! Don't allow sitting to dominate your day! It seems logical to me "action is better than inaction." Why? Because, when you sit and do nothing for an extended period-of-time, moving becomes even more difficult. When you sit and do nothing, you begin to worry; to focus on yourself. Your troubles seem to magnify. I'm no doctor. I'm just a gray-haired, granny that's speaking from personal experience.

Yesterday I got up, drank my morning coffee, hobbled to the bathroom, looked in the mirror and groaned. I groaned, not because my hair reminded me of comedienne, Phyllis Diller, which it did. I groaned, knowing I most likely had an entire day of sitting to look forward to. Grandson, Gus, had a hockey tournament in Saginaw, Michigan. He and his family were already there. For my

Action or Inaction?

hubby and I to get there would take almost three hours of driving and sitting in the car. Once there, we would sit for hours in an ice-cold arena.

Another grandson, Mack, had a basketball tournament in Antwerp, Ohio. That's two hours closer than Saginaw, but once again, this would be an entire day of bleacher-butt. I truly love to watch my grandkids participate, however, both scenarios seemed like a whole lot of sitting. I developed an alternate plan, and I needed to make some contacts.

I texted, Anita, mother of the basketball player, and offered to watch, Malone, her three-year-old. Then I texted, Ali, and offered to watch two-year-old Larkin, and four-year-old, Bo. Next, I called my mother-in-law, Louise, to see if she felt like meeting me and my giggling gang of wild wigglers at Johnson's, a familiar restaurant/craft store for lunch. She accepted the invitation. Things were looking up! This promised to be a good day, an action-filled day.

The grandkids were dropped off at my house, giving them time to play before it was time to go. Ohio winters make traveling with little ones a challenge. Bulky coats, gloves, and stocking caps are hard to put on "limp as a wet noodle" little bodies. After finally getting them bundled up, the next piece of the puzzle was to fit three car seats in a row, then reach around to get everyone safely buckled in. (This proved to be more strenuous than a Richard Simmons workout.) To keep the peace, I placed candy in the pudgy palm of each outstretched hand.

My mother-in-law met us at the designated time and place. After looking at all the lovely Christmas decorations (with kiddos finding it impossible not to touch) we quickly passed around the hand sanitizer and ordered lunch. The Country Cousins were thrilled to see their hotdogs already cut-up

Action or Inaction?

and placed on the plate as piggy faces with shredded cheddar cheese for hair. Before I finished my cup of soup, the hotdogs disappeared, and the three munchkins were begging for more. A second round of "piggy face" hotdogs was ordered.

A trip to the restroom couldn't be avoided. I ushered the two little princesses to the potty palace. There was a lot of "girl talk" pertaining to the delightfully decorated walls and the sweet-smelling soap. My mother-in-law held down the fort watching, Prince Bo, the lone survivor. Returning to our table we all pitched in to pick stray shredded cheese pieces off the floor. There was ice-cream for dessert, followed by hugs for great grandma, before we once again: bundled up, loaded up, and buckled up.

Overall, it was an exhausting day but a fun day! I was glad to hear both the hockey team and the basketball team won (despite my absence). I felt like I had won, too. I won by spending the day with people I love. I won by moving, not sitting. I won by feeling a sense of accomplishment. I won by focusing my attention on others.

If I'm to be completely honest, all that action and winning plum wore me out. Think I'll head to my recliner for a little inaction. (Everything in moderation is what I always say!)

Go With the Flow

I'VE FOUND THERE are times when it's necessary to consciously decide not to panic. Instead, take a deep breath, force yourself to relax, and go with the rhythm of life. In other words, just "Go with the flow." This past weekend was one of those times. I had the much-anticipated baptism of our sixth grandchild, Bo, written on my calendar for weeks, but somehow time slipped away. Since I volunteered to host the after-Christmas, after-church get-together, I now had only a couple of days to plan and prepare food for twenty-eight guests, shop for groceries, plus clean my neglected house.

How did this happen? How did the days and weeks fly by so fast? In my defense, there was the Hamler Heritage Society coffee cake sale, various Christmas gatherings, the Polar-Bear-Plunge at Hamilton Lake, breakfast at the Hamler Fire Station, a grandson's youth basketball game, another grandson's hockey game, morning coffee and doughnuts at Ron's in Deshler, shopping for flooring with my middle daughter, all mixed in with babysitting. I can't forget to mention the "must see" fifth season of "Downton Abbey." I decided not to worry. I'd just "Go with the flow."

Listing excuses makes me sound like I'm whining. I'm not. I'm simply saying, with all that I had going on, I felt unprepared for the next big event, our newest grandson's baptism. At the firemen's breakfast I was relating this dilemma to a friend. Her advice was, "Don't clean now, wait until everyone's gone." This fit into my current "Go with the flow" philosophy, so I seriously considered taking her advice. Following a closer inspection, I decided that might not be such a good idea.

Besides, I have a theory that's based on some "pretty horrifying" previous experiences. The one room, closet, or drawer you don't clean is precisely the one all guests will somehow manage to see. I started cleaning my bathroom's very messy makeup drawer. This activity immediately caught the interest of my five-year-old granddaughter, Meyta. This, in turn, sparked a creative "Go with the flow," idea. I gave her a sack and said, "Honey, you can take home anything you want from this drawer." In no time flat my drawer had a whole new empty, cleaned-out, mess-free look. One glance at my granddaughter's bulging sack, and I knew her mother, Anita, wouldn't be thanking me.

Barney's a senior dog that sleeps most of the day, and normally shows no interest in my house-cleaning agenda. However, when I switch on the vacuum, he magically turns into the energizer bunny. In a flash, he's off the couch, biting and barking at the sweeper as if he somehow lapped up water from Ponce de Leon's Fountain of Youth. With the noise of the sweeper and Barney's barking, I didn't hear my hubby come in and ask if there was anything he could do to help. I'm not buying it, but to this day he swears he really did come in and ask.

My husband's next appearance was to stick his head inside and inform me he scheduled an appointment for our car to get an oil change. "They're fitting us in right away so I need you to pick me up." In my book, this was less than perfect timing, but instead of getting upset, I chose to put down my dust rag, pack our granddaughter in her car seat, and "Go with the flow."

On the ride home I decided to make use of my captive audience. Stuck in the car with me, he couldn't escape to his office or hop in his pickup to go turn off the grain dryer.

Go With the Flow

So, during our return trip home, I recited his "honey do" list. This list included thaw out our frozen faucet, replace burned-out light bulbs, take out the garbage, put gas in the cars, and shovel snow off the front sidewalks. There's a definite feeling of satisfaction that comes with delegating responsibility.

By now I was in pretty good shape. All I had left was to cook the food, set up extra chairs, make sure my husband and I had clean clothes, and arrive at the baptism on time. I'm pleased to report everything at the church went without a hitch. Baptized baby, Bo, was a real trooper and didn't cry when cold baptismal water dampened his head. The other five Country Cousins sat relatively still with a little help from Tootsie Rolls, Smarties, and Goldfish.

Back at our house after the meal, the new parents, Ali and Rob, began opening congratulatory cards and gifts. "Whoops!" I whispered to my daughter. "Hope you don't mind that our present will be a little late." Her reply would make any mother proud. "Mom, that's OK. You've done a lot. Besides, I've learned from you to "Go with the flow." To which I said, "Amen!"

Soup Surprise!

IT'S THE TWILIGHT of December, and much like this book, the year is coming to its conclusion. Here in Ohio, we're entrenched in winter weather. The days are short, and evenings are long. The months of January and February sometimes seem to plod on forever! In my humble opinion, there's one thing that can help heighten the senses and satisfy the soul... I'm thinking soup!

I come from a soup loving family. When I was a kid, my father, (youngest Country Cousin, Ike's, namesake) was the one who concocted it. Most fathers like to stand at the grill and flip burgers. Mine liked to stand at the stove and stir soup. The aroma of boiling broth drifted through our home, and my father's voice did too. While the soup simmered, he sang. Unlike the Soup Nazi on "Seinfeld" reruns, Dad was never grumpy while making soup.

Thanks to Dad, I learned to make soups that satisfy. But my baking skills are sadly lacking. When asked to make cookies for bake sales, I'd buy cookies at the store, arrange them on a paper plate, cover them with clear wrap, and drop them off at the sale. The way I figured it; the cookies were freshly baked… just not by me. Once, someone asked for my cookie recipe. Then I had to fess up, "They're not homemade, they're store-made."

The bad news is, my baking's a bust, but the good news is, my soups can surprise! The soups I make are chicken noodle, vegetable beef, and dumpling. Chicken noodle is more than just a soup. In households across America, it's a home remedy for anyone feeling a bit "under the weather." If sipping chicken noodle soup doesn't cure you, at least it helps you feel less miserable. It's guaranteed to warm your tummy and clear your sinuses. An added bonus in my mind, all soups go great with potato chips!

Years ago, when I was a newlywed, I liked to attend auctions. When I got the final bid on an antique, white soup-urn, with accompanying lid, I thought I had a real treasure; something that would "dress up" my bland kitchen counter. The following week, I invited my grandma, Hilda Guelde, over for a soup-filled lunch.

I was about to ladle soup from the stove into my fancy, "new" antique urn, when Grandma, in a panicked voice ordered, "Konnie, STOP! Don't' put soup in that thing!" Seeing my startled reaction, she quickly went on to explain, "That's not for soup! That's an old-fashioned, um... well... it's a potty! Years ago we kept them in bedrooms... people used them at night and in the winter, making it easier to "go" inside, than to "go" outside to the outhouse.

My mouth dropped, and my face turned several shades of red. We both laughed quite a lot over that one! After I recovered from the shock, I thanked her for saving my soup (and the two of us) from a terrible fate. I assured Grandma, I had not used the portable, porcelain potty before this day. After she left, I quickly moved it from our kitchen to our attic, where it has remained ever since.

Several years ago, our daughter-in-law, Andrea, had a soup tasting party on New Year's Day. No, I didn't do the old "cookie caper," and open a can of soup, pour it in a crockpot and pass it off as homemade. The way I figured it, with my luck, somebody would want the recipe. What I brought was homemade dumpling soup, a family favorite and one my father taught me how to make. I've been thinking… maybe there are TWO

Soup Surprise!

things I can actually pass on to my Country Cousin grandkids - stories AND soups!

There's no clever way to end this crazy soup story. So, I'll simply borrow a quote from the world-famous Master Chef, Julia Child, and say, "Bon appetite!"

A Laughing Matter

With Thanksgiving and Christmas in the record books, our sights turn to welcoming in a new year. This is the time when people make pronouncements or resolutions; promises they intend to keep. I've never been a resolution type of gal, but this year is different. This year I resolve to laugh more. This past year, the situation with the coronavirus has made life more difficult for many people in many ways. As a result, I've noticed something missing in our daily lives. What's missing is laughter.

It's easy to take laughter for granted. Like the air we breathe, we assume laughter will always be there when we need it. Last year

I heard very little laughter outside of my immediate family group and my rambunctious Country Cousin grandkids. When life is tough, laughter may seem out of place, but perhaps it's during these tough times when we need laughter the most. Can you imagine a world without laughter? I can't, and I certainly wouldn't want to. I look at laughter as a special gift from God. Perhaps it's His way of lightening our load and easing our burdens.

Sure, there are times when life is difficult and circumstances so oppressive, all laughter is silenced. There are times in each person's life when a smile is impossible to muster, and laughter is unthinkable. There are times when laughter is inappropriate. Unfortunately, like discovering a buried diamond, laughter isn't always easy to find. But the good thing is, laughter is like riding a bike. Even after a long period without it, you never really forget how to do it.

A Laughing Matter

A good dose of laughter is healthy. Everyone is familiar with the saying, "An apple a day keeps the doctor away." I suggest it should be changed to, "A laugh a day keeps the doctor away." I'm convinced if we all laughed more, our mental and physical health would benefit. We'd live longer too, or at the very least, we'd be happier while we were alive. If "laughter is the best medicine," then maybe for some of our minor maladies, doctors should write a prescription, directing us to watch a comedy. Who knows, an old Abbot and Costello film just might speed up recovery.

What makes us laugh? Something that happens out of the ordinary or unexpectedly might "tickle our ribs." When I was a young girl, while visiting my brother and sister-in-law, I got the giggles. With tears streaming down my cheeks I couldn't stop laughing. All because, in my attempt to cut a really tough pork chop, my fork slipped, causing the entire chop to flip in the air and land "kerplop" on my lap. Contrary to popular belief, laughter isn't always catching. Nobody else at the supper table saw humor in my mishap. "I was the lone laugher!"

Sometimes relief makes us laugh. Our then, three-year-old son, Ryan, was supposed to go to the front of the church to hear the children's sermon. As he walked down the middle aisle, we noticed he was severely hunched over! My husband and I whispered our concern. Perhaps he had a stomach ailment, and we would soon be rushing him to emergency. I suggested he had a spinal issue that had previously gone undetected.

To our chagrin, he returned to our pew, walking in the same alarming, doubled-over manner. We immediately asked what was wrong, and chuckled with relief after hearing his answer. He told us his shirt button was twisted and stuck in his belt buckle, making it impossible for him to straighten up.

A Laughing Matter

Some things aren't funny at the time, but make you laugh years later. One summer, when my Aunt Leona was visiting from Texas, she decided to take her car through the automatic car wash. She had never done this before and turned her steering wheel instead of keeping it straight, causing the car to jump off the track.

There was no attendant on duty, so she panicked and drove on out, scraping the entire side of her car the whole way through. At the time, she was understandably shaken and upset, but a few years later she joked and laughed as we teased her about the time she "crashed through the car wash."

Young kids often resort to acting silly to make adults laugh. When they get the desired results, they wrongly think those same actions will continue to keep everyone in stitches. My mother, Anita, (namesake of our middle daughter) had a saying that quickly taught me when to stop the attention-getting antics. "First times laughy, second times smiley, third times spanky."

Yep, this past year has been tough on everybody. I resolve to laugh more this coming new year, and with all nine Country Cousins living within a short distance of my husband and me, I'm pretty sure I can make that happen. Of course, there are no guarantees, but I do know kids like jokes, so the next time I see, Mack, Gus, Evie, Meyta, Cece, Bo, Malone, Larkin, or Ike, I'll say, "Hey, kiddos, since Coronavirus was a big problem during last year's Thanksgiving and Christmas, what had to be the most popular side dish served at almost every meal in America? MASKed potatoes!"

P.S. Go ahead, see if this joke works on your munchkins too. I'll keep my fingers and toes crossed that at least a muffled snicker is the result.

P.P.S. Thank you for allowing me to share my special holiday memories. Here's wishing you all a safe and health-filled new year, one that's packed full of family stories, fellowship, and laughter!

CPSIA information can be obtained
at www.ICGtesting.com
Printed in the USA
FSHW011523141021